The Amazing Liver Cleanse

The Amazing Liver Cleanse

A POWERFUL TOOL TO IMPROVE YOUR HEALTH

by

Andreas Moritz

ISBN 1-58500-353-0

ABOUT THE BOOK

Andreas Moritz addresses th13e most common but rarely cause of illness – gallstones congesting the liver. Twenty million Americans suffer from attacks of gallstones every year. In many cases, treatment consists of removing the gall bladder, at the cost of $5 billion a year. Yet many more Americans, including most people suffering a chronic illness such as heart disease, arthritis, MS, cancer, or diabetes, have hundreds if not thousands of gallstones (mainly clumps of hardened bile) blocking the bile ducts of the liver.

This book provides a thorough understanding of what causes gallstones in the liver and gall bladder and how gallstones in turn become the major cause of illness prevalent in modern societies. It provides the reader with the knowledge how to recognise them and gives the necessary do-it-yourself instructions on how to remove them painlessly and in the comfort of one's home. It also gives practical guidelines as to how to prevent new stones from being formed – an essential part in any program

To all those wishing to take responsibility for their own health and happiness

For Reasons of Legality

First Edition 1998
Second edition 1999

CONTENTS

INTRODUCTION

Most people believe that gallstones can be found only in the gall bladder. This is a false assumption. Most gallstones are actually formed in the liver and only a few in the gall bladder. This statement can easily be verified by anyone who gives himself a liver cleanse, regardless of whether he is a layperson, a medical doctor, a scientist, and someone who no longer has a gall bladder and is believed to be free of gallstones altogether.

An estimated 20% of the world's population will develop gallstones in their gall bladder at some stage in their lives. This figure, however, does not account for the many more people who will develop gallstones in the liver. From my personal experience as a health practitioner with thousands of patients suffering all types of diseases, I can document that each one of them has had large amounts of gallstones in the liver. Surprisingly, only relatively few of them have had a history of gallstones in the gall bladder. Gallstones in the liver are, as will be seen in this book, the main obstacle to maintaining health, youthfulness, and vitality. They are indeed one of the major reasons why people fall ill and have difficulty in recuperating from an illness.

The failure to recognise gallstones in the liver may be an important missing link in the field of medicine, both orthodox and complementary. By understanding how gallstones in the liver contribute to the development of almost every type of disease and by taking the simple steps of removing these obstructions, every person can discover for himself an easy method to restore health on a permanent basis. The implications of applying the liver cleanse for yourself or, if you are a health practitioner, for your patients, are both vast and rewarding. To have a clean liver is like having a clean start in life.

The liver is the major controlling agent of normal growth

and healthy functioning of all body cells are. Any malfunction, deficiency, or abnormal growth pattern of the cell is to a large extent due to an impaired liver performance. There is rarely a disease in the body that does not start in the liver.

All diseases or symptoms of ill health are caused by obstruction. If a blocked blood vessel no longer allows delivery of vital oxygen or nutrients to a group of cells, the cells will be forced to introduce emergency measures or specific survival tactics. Many of the cells will not survive the 'famine', others will learn to mutate and live off other cells and toxic materials, which may turn them malignant or cancerous.

A constipated colon will prevent the body from eliminating the waste products contained in the faeces. If a stone begins to obstruct the flow of urine in the urinary system, kidney infection or even kidney failure may result. If hardened mucous blocks the air passages of the lungs, we literally run out of breath. The thickening of blood or its restricted flow through the arteries can lead to many problems in the body, including skin diseases, arthritis, heart attacks and strokes.

Any such or similar obstruction in the body is directly and indirectly linked to an impaired liver performance and in particular to a blockage caused by gallstones both in the liver and in the gall bladder. The presence of stones in these organs greatly impairs the digestion of food, elimination of waste, and detoxification of harmful substances in the blood. By unblocking the liver and gall bladder, the body's 60-100 trillion cells will be able to 'breathe' more oxygen, receive more nutrients, eliminate their metabolic waste products more efficiently, and maintain perfect communication links with the nervous system, endocrine system and all other parts of the body.

Although almost every patient with a chronic illness has an excessively large number of gallstones in the liver (this can easily be verified by having a liver cleanse), unless there is a specific liver disease, this important organ is rarely considered a 'culprit.' Since the majority of gallstones in the liver and gall bladder consist of the same 'harmless' constituents as are contained in liquid *bile* with cholesterol being their main ingredient, they are 'invisible' to X-ray technologies. Stones in the liver don't *show up* as solid whereas some of the gallstones (20 per cent) occurring in the gall bladder can be made up entirely of minerals, mainly calcium salts and bile pigment. Modern diagnostic tools can easily detect these hardened and relatively large stones but fail to recognise the softer and smaller ones in the liver. Only when there are excessive amounts of large stones in the liver can an ultrasound reveal a *"fatty liver."* In such case the ultrasound pictures show a liver that looks almost completely white (instead of dark). A *fatty liver* can have up to 6,000- 8,000 stones before it succumbs to suffocation and ceases to function.

But even if the early stages of a *fatty liver* are recognised and diagnosed through ultrasound, this vital organ is hardly ever relieved of the heavy burden it has to "carry" by having accumulated hundreds and, in many cases, thousands of these hardened bile deposits which continuously block the liver's *bile ducts*. In view of the effect the stones have on liver performance as a whole, it is irrelevant whether the stones consist of mainly thickened cholesterol or are mineralised and hard. Whether we call them gallstones, fat deposits or clots consisting of hardened bile, the net result is that they prevent bile from flowing through the bile ducts.

Bile is a green coloured, alkaline fluid with many functions. Apart from helping the digestion of fat, calcium, and protein foods, it is needed to maintain normal fat levels in the blood, to remove toxins from the liver, to help maintain proper acid/alkaline balance in the intestinal tract, and to keep the colon from breeding harmful microbes. To maintain a strong and healthy digestive system and to feed the body the right amount of nutrients, the liver has to produce between 1 and 1 ½ quarts (1,1 -1,6 litres) of *bile* a day. Anything less than that (many people produce just about a cup full) is bound to cause problems with the digestion of food, elimination of waste and constant need for detoxifying the blood. Almost all health problems are a direct consequence of reduced or blocked *bile* production and inefficient *bile* transport.

People with chronic illnesses often have thousands of gallstones congesting the *bile* ducts of the liver. Some stones may have impacted the gall bladder as well. By removing the stones through a series of liver cleanses, and subsequently maintaining a healthy diet and lifestyle, the liver and gall bladder will be able to restore their natural efficiency, and most symptoms of discomfort or disease in the body will begin to subside. Allergies will lessen or disappear, back pain will dissipate, and energy and well being will improve dramatically. Cleansing the liver *bile* ducts from gallstones is one of the most important and powerful procedures to improve your health.

In this book you will learn how to painlessly remove hundreds of gallstones which can range from the size of a pinhead to the size of a walnut. The actual cleanse takes place within a period of less than 14 hours and can conveniently be taken over a weekend at home. This book further explains why gallstones blocking the *bile* ducts both inside and outside the liver can be considered to be the main cause of every major or minor illness. You will also find out the signs or marks that indicate the presence of stones in the liver or gall bladder. Other sections of the book deal with the possible causes of gallstones and how to prevent new ones from being formed. 'What can I expect from a liver cleanse' will cover some of the possible health benefits of this profound self-help programme. The question and answer section deals with any queries you may have about the cleanse.

Chapter 1

The Liver Cleanse

Cleansing the liver and gall bladder from gallstones is one of the most important and powerful tools to improve your health. To remove gallstones you need the following things:

Apple juice	6-12 one litre boxes
Epsom salts	4 tablespoons
Olive oil, cold-pressed and pure	half cup
Fresh grapefruit (pink is best)	enough to squeeze 2/3 cup of juice
Black Walnut Hull Tincture	10 drops
2 pint jars, one with a lid	

Note: 1. The 10 drops of Black Walnut Hull Tincture recommended in the cleanse recipe are used to kill any parasites that may come out of the *bile* ducts during the cleanse (if you can't find it or are allergic to it, you may replace it with 10 drops of tincture made from cloves or chew on 2-3 cloves straight after drinking the mixture of olive oil and grapefruit juice).

2. If you cannot tolerate grapefruit juice or if it tends to make you nauseous you may use freshly squeezed lemon and orange juice (1/3rd cup each) instead.

Preparation

• Drink 1 litre of packaged apple juice a day for a period of six days. This will soften the stones and make their passage through the bile ducts easier. The apple juice has a strong cleansing effect and may cause some bloating and even diarrhoea during the first few days. The fermentation of the juice helps the expansion of the bile ducts. If this becomes somewhat uncomfortable, mix the apple juice with water. Drink the juice slowly throughout the day, in between meals (**avoid** during, just before and two hours after meals, and in the evening). This is in addition to your normal water intake. Eat normal but light meals. **Note:** packaged apple juice (possibly of organic source), although normally not recommended, works well for the cleanse.

• The main part of the liver cleanse is best done over a weekend, when you have enough time to rest, and preferably during the days of full moon or waning moon. While being on the cleanse avoid taking any medicine, vitamins, or pills that are not absolutely necessary.

• On the sixth day of drinking apple juice, if you feel hungry in the morning, eat a light breakfast such as cooked cereal, fruit or fruit juice (no milk, butter, yoghurt cheese, ham, eggs, etc.). For lunch eat plain cooked vegetables with rice and a little salt (no protein foods and no butter or oil). Don't eat or drink anything (except water) after 2 PM! The timing given below is essential for the success of the cleanse.

Doing the Cleanse

<u>Evening</u>

6:00 PM: Mix four tablespoons of Epsom salts in 3 cups of water and keep it in a jar. This makes four servings, ¾ cup or 185 ml each. Drink your first portion now. You may take a few sips of water afterwards to get rid of the bitter taste in the mouth (it may be easier to take it with a large plastic straw, as this bypasses the taste buds on the tongue).

8:00 PM: Drink your second ¾ cup of Epsom salts.

9:30 PM: If you haven't had a bowel movement until now, take a water enema; this will trigger a series of bowel movements.

9:45 PM: Squeeze the grapefruits (or lemons and oranges); you will need ¾ cup of juice; remove pulp. Pour the juice and ½ cup olive oil into the pint jar. Add the 10 drops of Black Walnut Hull Tincture. Close the jar tightly and shake hard about twenty times or until watery. You want to drink this mixture at 10pm, but if still feel you will need to visit the bathroom a few more times, you may delay for 10 minutes.

10:00 PM: Stand next to your bed (don't sit) and drink the concoction, if possible in one go or otherwise with a large plastic straw. Don't take more than 5 minutes for this.

LIE DOWN STRAIGHT AWAY, this is necessary to help release the gallstones! Turn off the lights and lie flat on your back with your head up high on a pillow or two. Put your attention on your liver and, if you can, visualise the mixture moving the stones out of the numerous bile ducts in your liver. *Keep perfectly still for at least 20 minutes!* This gives the stones a chance to move along the bile ducts. There won't be any pain because the Epsom salts will keep the bile duct valves wide open. Go to sleep if you can.

If at any time during the night you feel the urge to have a bowel movement, do so. Check if there are already small gallstones (pea green or tan coloured ones) floating in the toilet. You may feel nauseous during the night and early morning hours. This will pass as the morning progresses.

The Following Morning

6:00 - 6:30 AM: Upon awakening, but not before 6am, drink your third ¾ cup of Epsom salts (if you feel very thirsty drink a glass of warm water before taking the salts). Rest or meditate. If you are sleepy, you may go back to bed, although it is best if the body stays in the upright position.

8:00 - 8:30 AM: Drink your fourth and last ¾ cup of Epsom salts and rest.

10:00 - 10:30 AM: You may drink freshly pressed fruit juice, preferably apple or orange juice.

Half an hour later eat 1-2 pieces of fruit. One hour later you may eat regular (but light) food.

The Results you can expect

You will have a number of bowel movements in the form of diarrhoea, consisting of gallstones mixed first with food residue and then with only water. Most of the gallstones float in the toilet because they contain large amounts of cholesterol. You will see mostly green ones of all sizes and shapes, some are pea-sized or smaller, and others are as big as 2-3 centimetres. There may be hundreds of stones coming out at once. Also watch out for tan coloured and white ones. Some of the larger tan coloured stones may sink with the stool because they are calcified and contain heavier toxic substances and only small amounts of cholesterol. All the green stones are as soft as putty, thanks to the apple juice.

You may also find a layer of white or tan coloured scum or 'foam' floating in the toilet. The foam consists of millions of tiny white, sharp-edged cholesterol crystals, which can easily rupture small bile ducts; they are equally important to get rid of

It is most likely that some stones will get caught in the colon. They can quickly be removed through colonic irrigation. If they remain in the colon, they can cause irritation, headaches and abdominal discomfort. If colonics are not available where you live, you can take a coffee enema followed by a water enema. This, however, doesn't guarantee that all the remaining stones are removed. There is no real substitute for colonic irrigation (for more details on colonics and enemas see the book "The Key to Health and Rejuvenation.)

Try to make a rough estimate of how many stones you have eliminated. To permanently cure bursitis, back pain, allergies, or other health problems, and to prevent diseases from arising you need to remove **all** the stones. This may require up to six or more cleanses which can be performed at 2-3 week intervals (don't cleanse more frequently than that). If you cannot cleanse this often, you may take more time between the cleanses. The important thing to remember is that once you have started cleansing the liver keep cleansing it until no more stones come out. Leaving it half clean for a long period of time (three or more months) can cause greater discomfort than not cleansing it at all.

The liver as a whole will begin to function more efficiently soon after the first cleanse and you may notice sudden improvements, sometimes within a few hours. Pains will be less, energy will increase and clarity of mind will improve considerably.

However, within a few days, stones from the rear of the liver will have travelled "forward" towards the two main bile ducts exiting the liver, which may cause some of the previous symptoms of discomfort to return. In fact, you might feel disappointed because the recovery seems so short-lived. But all this shows that there are still stones left behind, ready to be removed with the next round of elimination. Nevertheless, the liver's self-repair and cleansing responses will have increased significantly, adding a great deal of effectiveness to this all-important organ of the body.

As long as there are still a few small stones moving from some of the thousands of small bile ducts towards the hundreds of larger bile ducts, they may combine to form larger stones and produce such previously experienced symptoms as backache, headache, earache, digestive trouble, bloating, irritability, anger, etc., although these may be less severe than they were before. If a new cleanse no longer produces any stones, which usually happens after the sixth cleanse, your liver can considered to be in excellent condition. Still, it is recommended to repeat the liver cleanse every six months. Each cleanse will give a further boost to the liver and take care of any toxins that may have accumulated in the meanwhile. **Note:** Never cleanse when you are a suffering an acute illness, even if it is just a simple cold.

Making the Liver Cleanse more Effective

A more effective version of the liver cleanse includes taking one table spoon of pure, cold pressed olive oil mixed with 1 table spoon of lemon juice on an empty stomach in the morning, during the six days of preparation. Start by drinking one or two glasses of warm water first thing in the morning and wait for 10-15 minutes. Mix the oil with the lemon juice until watery and drink. You may have breakfast after one hour. Although the liver cleanse is very effective without this addition to the pre-treatment, it can add more success to the cleanse. If your body does not agree with the oil, you may instead eat two medium sweet pears on an empty stomach in the morning, at least ½ hour before eating breakfast.

Although the liver cleanse by itself can produce dramatic results, for maximum benefit it is best done *after* a colon and kidney cleanse. Cleansing the colon and the kidneys first will ensure that the stones and toxins coming out of the liver are more easily eliminated without causing too much extra burden on the vital organs of elimination. The ideal pre-treatment for the first liver cleanse consists of 2-3 sessions of *colonic irrigation*, which is best preceded by 3-4 weeks of cleansing the kidneys.

Removing gallstones from the liver and gallbladder may leave some of the stones and other toxic residues in the colon. It is therefore very important that you have a colonic after each liver cleanse. To give the best possible results, the colonic should be taken within three days after the cleanse. Also, drinking one cup of any kidney/bladder tea ½ hour before meals for three days after each cleanse helps the kidneys to dispose of any harmful substances that may have moved there as a result of the liver cleanse.

Chapter 2

Gallstones in the Liver – A Major Health Risk

Think of the liver as a huge city with thousands of houses, streets, water, oil, and gas pipes, sewage systems, power lines, factories, shops, transport systems, etc. The city is organised in such a way that it can provide for everything that its inhabitants require to sustain their lives. Should the city life be paralysed by strike actions, failing power supply or devastating earthquake the population will begin to suffer shortcomings on every level.

With all its hundreds of different functions and connection to all parts of the body, the liver processes, produces and supplies every possible nutrient to the 60-100 trillion inhabitants of the body – the cells. Each cell of the body is in itself a microscopic city of immense complexity, which receives the nutrients it requires for its numerous activities from the liver. With its intricate labyrinth of veins, ducts and specialised cells the liver needs to be free of any interference or obstruction in order to maintain a problem-free production line and frictionless distribution system throughout the body.

Because the liver is the main organ responsible for processing, converting, distributing and maintaining the body's 'fuel' supply, obstructive gallstones can greatly impair its capacity to deliver the right amount of nutrients and energy to the right places at the right time. This can upset the very delicate balance in the body, i.e., homeostasis, and disrupt any of its systems and organs. Freeing the liver and gall bladder from all stones not only helps to restore balance and set the precondition for the body to heal itself but is perhaps one of the best precautions one can take to protect oneself against illness in the future.

If you suffer any of the following symptoms or similar ones you are likely to have numerous gallstones in your liver and gall bladder:

Low appetite, food cravings, any digestive disorder, diarrhoea, constipation, clay coloured stools, hernia, flatulence, haemorrhoids, dull pain on the right side, difficulty with breathing, liver cirrhosis, hepatitis and many other types of infection, high cholesterol, *pancreatitis, heart disease, brain disorders, duodenal ulcers, nausea and vomiting, a 'bilious' or angry personality, impotence and other sexual problems, prostate diseases, urinary problems, hormonal imbalances, menstrual and menopausal disorders, problems with vision, puffy eyes, skin disorders, liver spots especially on the back of the hands and facial area, dizziness and fainting, loss of muscle tone, excessive weight or wasting, strong shoulder and back pain, a pain at the top of the shoulder blade, dark colour under the eyes, morbid complexion, the tongue is glossy or covered with a white or yellow coat, scoliosis, gout, frozen shoulder, stiff neck, asthma, headaches and migraines, tooth and gum problems, yellowness of the eyes and skin, sciatica, numbness and paralysis of legs, joint diseases, knee problems, osteoporosis, obesity, chronic fatigue, kidney diseases, cancer, MS, ME, Alzheimer's disease, cold extremities, excessive heat and perspiration in the upper part of the body, very greasy hair, etc.*

The Importance of Bile

One of the liver's most important functions is to produce *bile* (1 to 1 ½ quarts a day), a bitter, sour fluid which is highly alkaline. Food cannot be digested without *bile*. To enable the small intestines to absorb fat and calcium from food it must first be mixed with *bile*. When fat isn't absorbed it shows that *bile* secretion is insufficient. The fat stays in the intestines and since it is lighter than water, it makes the stool float. If fat isn't absorbed then calcium isn't absorbed either leaving the blood in a deficit. The blood subsequently takes its extra calcium from the bones.

Apart from breaking down fatty acids contained in our food, *bile* also removes toxins from the liver and de-acidifies and purifies the intestines. If *gallstones have seriously impeded the bile flow in the liver or gall bladder*, the colour of the stool may be tan, orange-yellow or pale as in clay, instead of greenish-brown. Gallstones are an *effect* of an unhealthy diet and life-style. Even if all other disease-causing factors are eliminated but gallstones are still present in the liver, they remain a *root cause* for future illness. For this reason, the subject of gallstones has been included here as a major risk factor or cause of disease. The following sections outline some of the harmful consequences that gallstones in the liver have on various parts and systems of the body. Removing the stones restores their normal and healthy functioning.

Disorders of the Digestive System

There are four main activities in the alimentary tract of our digestive system: *Ingestion, Digestion, Absorption and Elimination.* The alimentary canal begins at the mouth, passes through the thorax, abdomen and pelvis region and ends at the anus. When food is ingested a series of digestive processes begin which can be divided into the *mechanical* breakdown of food by *mastication* (chewing) and *chemical* breakdown by *enzymes* present in the secretions produced by glands of the digestive system. (Enzymes are minute chemical substances that cause, or speed up chemical changes in other substances without themselves being changed. Digestive enzymes are contained in the saliva of the salivary glands of the mouth, the gastric juice in the stomach, the intestinal juice in the small intestine, the pancreatic juice in the pancreas and the *bile* in the liver).

Absorption is the process by which tiny nutrient particles of digested food pass through the intestinal walls into the blood and lymph vessels for distribution to the cells of the body. The bowels excrete whatever food substances cannot be digested or absorbed as faeces. Faeces also contain bile from the liver, which carries the waste products resulting from the breakdown (catabolism) of red blood cells, and large number of microbes. Health is the result of the smooth and balanced functioning of each of these major activities. On the other hand, disease results when one or more of these functions are impaired. The presence of gallstones in the liver and gall bladder has a strong disruptive influence on the digestion and absorption of food and on the elimination of waste.

Diseases of the Mouth

Gallstones in the liver are also responsible for most diseases that occur in the mouth. Bacterial infection **(thrush)** or viral infection **(herpes)** result when due to poor digestion and absorption of food, toxic waste is not sufficiently excreted which impairs immunity and permits bacteria and viruses to infect various parts of the body, including the mouth. Gallstones harbour plenty of bacteria and viruses, which escape the liver with the secretion of *bile* and infect parts of the body, which have the least resistance to them.

In addition, the presence of gallstones in the liver inhibits proper *bile* secretion, which in turns reduces appetite, and secretion of saliva from the salivary glands in the mouth. Hence there is no adequate flow of saliva, which is necessary to cleanse the mouth and keep its tissues soft and pliable. Harmful bacteria begin to invade the mouth cavity, which can even lead to tooth decay. A bitter taste in the mouth is caused by *bile* that has moved from the gall bladder into the stomach and up into the mouth. This drastically alters the pH value of saliva, which impairs its cleansing properties, making the mouth susceptible to infection.

If there is ulceration in the lower lip, this indicates a simultaneous inflammatory process in the large intestine.

Repeated occurrence of **mouth ulcers** in the corners of the mouth show the presence of **duodenal ulcers**. **Tongue ulcers,** depending on their location on the tongue, indicate inflammatory processes in corresponding areas of the alimentary canal.

Diseases of the Stomach

Gallstones can lead to regurgitation of *bile* acids and salts into the stomach, which changes the composition and amount of mucus that protects the surface stomach lining from the destructive effects of hydrochloric acid. This condition, known as *gastritis* can be acute or chronic. When the surface cells (epithelium) of the stomach are exposed to acid gastric juice the cells absorb hydrogen ions, which increases their internal acidity, counterbalances their basic metabolic processes and leads to an inflammatory reaction. In more severe cases there may be ulceration of the *mucosa (peptic ulcer),* bleeding, perforation of the stomach wall and *peritonitis,* a condition when an ulcer erodes through the full thickness of the stomach or duodenum and their contents enter the peritoneal cavity.

All other known causes of gastritis such as excessive alcohol consumption, heavy cigarette smoking, drinking coffee every day, X-radiation and cytotoxic drugs, aspirin and other anti-inflammatory drugs, food poisoning, very spicy foods, bacteria, dehydration, stress, etc., also cause gallstones in the liver and gall bladder, adding more complications. In the final event, there may be a formation of malignant tumours.

Trying to combat the bug, which is believed to cause stomach ulcers through antibiotic drugs may give temporary relief, but it cannot cure the condition. Once drug intake is discontinued the bug returns. Gallstones harbour these bugs and regurgitating *bile* takes them into the stomach where they cause re-infection. Most stomach disorders disappear spontaneously when all gallstones from the liver and gall bladder are removed and a healthy diet and life-style is maintained on a regular basis.

Diseases of the Pancreas

The pancreas is a small gland with its head lying in the curve of the duodenum. Its main duct joins the common *bile* duct (of the liver and gall bladder) to form what is known as the *ampulla of the bile duct*. The *ampulla* enters the duodenum at its midpoint. Apart from secreting the hormones *insulin* and *glucagon,* the pancreas produces *pancreatic juice* containing enzymes that digest carbohydrates, proteins, and fats. When acid stomach contents enter the duodenum they are mixed with pancreatic juice and *bile* which creates the proper pH (acid/alkali balance) at which the pancreatic enzymes are most effective (both *bile* and pancreatic juice are highly alkaline)

Gallstones in the liver or gall bladder can reduce the secretion of *bile* from over a quart to as little as a cup full of *bile* a day which severely disrupts the digestive process, particularly if fats or fat containing foods have been consumed. Subsequently, the pH is not raised high enough, which inhibits the action of the pancreatic enzymes as well as those secreted by the small intestines leaving the food only partially digested. Improperly digested food, saturated with stomach acid, can have a toxic and irritating effect on the entire intestinal tract.

If a gallstone has moved from the gall bladder into the ampulla, where the common *bile* duct and the pancreatic ducts meet, the release of pancreatic juice becomes obstructed and *bile* begins to move into the pancreas. The result is that protein-splitting pancreatic enzymes, which are normally activated only in the duodenum, are activated while still in the pancreas. These enzymes begin to digest parts of pancreatic tissue, which can lead to infection, suppuration and **local thrombosis**. This condition is known as **pancreatitis**.

Regular obstruction of the ampulla by gallstones releases inherent bacteria, viruses and toxins into the pancreas which can cause further damage to pancreatic cells and eventually lead to malignant tumours. They occur mostly in the head of the pancreas, which obstructs the flow of *bile* and pancreatic juice. **Jaundice** often develops as well.

Gallstones in the liver, gall bladder and ampulla may also be responsible for both types of *diabetes* -- insulin-dependent and non-insulin-dependent. All patients of mine with diabetes, including children, have had large quantities of stones in their liver. Each liver cleanse further improved their condition, provided they followed a healthy regimen as well.

Diseases of the Liver

The liver is the largest gland in the body and weighs up to 3 pounds. It is suspended behind the ribs on the upper right side of the abdomen and spans almost the entire width of the body. The liver is an extremely active organ with hundreds of different functions.

Because the liver is responsible for processing, converting, distributing, and maintaining the body's 'fuel' supply, i.e., nutrients and energy, gallstones impeding these functions may have a detrimental effect on the health of the liver and the rest of the body. The liver produces cholesterol as well as hormones and proteins that affect the way the body functions, grows and heals. It makes new amino acids and converts existing ones into proteins -- the building blocks of the cells, hormones, neurotransmitters, genes, etc. It also breaks down old cells, recycles the iron and stores many vitamins and nutrients. Gallstones disrupt all these functions.

Apart from breaking down alcohol, the liver also detoxifies noxious substances, bacteria, parasites, and certain drug compounds. It uses specific enzymes to convert the wastes or poison into substances that can be safely carried out of the body. The liver filters more than a quart of blood each minute. Gallstones in the liver's *bile* ducts impair this important function, which can lead to **liver diseases.**

All liver diseases are preceded by extensive *bile* duct obstruction through gallstones which distort the structural framework of the liver *lobules* which are the main units composing the liver (there are about 50,000 of such units in the liver). Subsequently, blood circulation to and from the liver cells as well as *bile* secretion by the liver cells becomes increasingly impeded. Nerve fibres become damaged, too. This will eventually damage or destroy liver cells and their *lobules*. There is a gradual replacement of damaged cells by fibrous tissue, causing further obstructions and an increase of pressure on the liver's blood vessels. If the regeneration of liver cells does not keep pace with damage, liver failure is imminent.

Acute *hepatitis* results when whole groups of liver cells die. Gallstones harbour large quantities of viruses, which can invade and infect liver cells, causing degenerative changes. As gallstones increase in size and number and more cells become infected and die entire *lobules* (liver units) begin to collapse and blood vessels begin to develop *kinks*. The resulting interference with the circulation of blood to the remaining liver cells causes further damage. The effect of these changes on the overall performance of the liver largely depends on the extent of obstruction caused by gallstones in the liver *bile* ducts. Cancer of the liver can only occur after many years of progressive occlusion of the liver's *bile* ducts. This applies also to tumours in the liver that emanate from primary tumours in the gastrointestinal tract, the lungs, or the breast (see section on cancer).

Most **liver infections** (type A, type B, and type non-A and type non-B) occur when a certain number of liver *lobules* are congested with gallstones, which can happen from very early age. A healthy liver and immune system is able to destroy incoming virus material, whether it is picked up from the environment or through blood, without falling ill. Gallstones can pick up plenty of live viruses. Once they are released into the blood they can cause chronic of hepatitis. Non viral infections of the liver are caused by bacteria that are spread from any of the *bile* ducts obstructed by gallstones.

The presence of gallstones in the *bile* ducts also impairs the liver cell's ability to deal with toxic substances such as chloroform, cytotoxic drugs, anabolic steroids, alcohol, aspirin, fungi, food additives, etc., which develops hypersensitivity to these predictable toxic substances and other unpredictable toxic substances contained in many medicinal drugs.

The most common form of **jaundice** results when

gallstones and fibrous tissue that have distorted the structural framework of liver *lobules* obstruct the movement of *bile* through the *bile* channels and the liver cells can no longer conjugate and excrete *bile* pigment (*bilirubin*). *Bilirubin* concentration in the blood may be three times above normal before the yellow coloration of the skin and the conjunctiva of the eyes is evident. Unconjugated bilirubin has a toxic effect on brain cells. Jaundice may also be caused by a tumour in the head of the pancreas (see diseases of the pancreas).

Diseases of the Gall bladder and Bile Ducts

The gall bladder is a pear-shaped sac attached to the posterior side of the liver (see illustration below). The liver secretes *bile*, which passes into the gall bladder where mucus is added and water absorbed to make it more concentrated. The muscular walls of the gall bladder contract and expel *bile* when food from the stomach enters the duodenum. A more marked activity is noted if food (chyme) entering the duodenum contains a high proportion of fat.

Gallstones consist of deposits of the constituents of *bile*, i.e., *bile*, *bile* salts, *bile* pigment, water, mucus and cholesterol, as well as toxins, bacteria, and sometimes-dead parasites. Typically, stones within the gall bladder grow in size for about 8 years before symptoms begin to occur. The large stones are generally calcified and *can* be detected easily radiologically or by using ultrasonography. Around 85% of gallstones found in the gall bladder measure about 2 cm across. They are formed when, due to factors explained in chapter 4, *bile* in the gall bladder becomes saturated and the bile's constituents that can't be absorbed, harden.

If a stone is expelled by the gall bladder and becomes impacted in the *cystic bile duct* or the *common bile duct*, there is very strong spasmodic contraction of the wall of the duct to try to move the stone onwards. This causes severe pain known as *biliary colic* and **distension of the gall bladder**. When the gall bladder is packed with gallstones, it too goes into extremely painful spasmodic muscle contractions. Gallstones can cause irritation and inflammation of the lining of the gall bladder and the cystic and common *bile* ducts. This is known as **cholecystitis.** There may also be superimposed microbial infection. **Ulceration** of the tissues between the gall bladder and the duodenum or colon with **fistula formation**, and later **fibrous adhesions**, are not uncommon either.

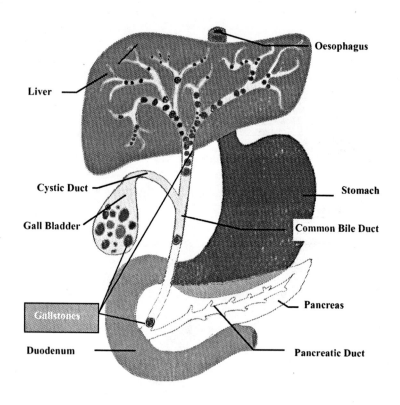

Illustration: Gallstones in the Liver and Gall Bladder

Gall bladder diseases generally originate in the liver. When liver lobules become distorted through gallstones and eventually through fibrous tissue, then venous pressure rises in the portal vein. This in turn increases the pressure in the cystic vein, which drains venous blood from the gall bladder into the portal vein. As a result, gall bladder functions become impaired and gallstones are formed.

Intestinal Diseases

The small intestine is continuous with the stomach at the *pyloric sphincter* and has a length of 5-6 metres. It leads into the large intestines, which are about 1,5 metres long. The small intestine secretes intestinal juices to complete digestion of carbohydrates, protein, and fats, protects against infection by microbes that have survived the antimicrobial action of hydrochloric acid in the stomach, and absorbs nutrient materials necessary for nourishing and maintaining the body.

When acid *chyme* from the stomach enters the duodenum it is mixed first with *bile* and *pancreatic juice* and then with *intestinal juice*. Gallstones in the liver and gall bladder drastically reduce secretion of *bile*, which diminishes the ability of pancreatic *enzymes* to digest carbohydrates, protein, and fat. This inhibits the small intestine from properly absorbing the nutrient components of these foods, i.e.: *monosaccharides* from carbohydrates, *amino acids* from protein, and *fatty acids* and *glycerol* from fats.

Since the presence of *bile* in the intestines is essential for the absorption of digested fats, calcium and vitamin K, gallstones can lead to life threatening diseases, such as **heart disease, osteoporosis,** and **cancer**. Vitamin K is necessary for the formation by the liver of the compounds responsible for the clotting of blood; in case of a deficiency, **haemorrhagic disease** may result. Calcium is essential for the hardening of bone and teeth, the coagulation of blood, and the mechanism of muscle contraction. In addition, vitamin A and carotene are only absorbed from the small intestine satisfactorily if fat absorption is normal. If vitamin A absorption is insufficient, the *epithelial* cells, which are an essential part of all the organs, blood vessels, lymph vessels, etc. in the body, become damaged. Vitamin A is necessary to maintain healthy eyes and protect against or reduce microbial infection.

Improperly digested foods in the small and large intestines tend to ferment and putrefy which can lead to irritation of the mucous lining, and impair the immune system, 60% of which is located in the intestines. Incapable of dealing effectively with the massive amount of toxins generated by harmful microbes trying to break down improperly digested foods, the small and large intestines may be afflicted with a number of disorders including **diarrhoea, constipation, abdominal gas, Chrohn's disease, ulcerative colitis, diverticular disease, hernias, dysentery, appendicitis, volvulus, intussusception, as well as benign and malignant tumours.**

Adequate *bile* flow maintains good digestion and absorption of food and has a strong cleansing action throughout the intestinal tract. Gallstones in the liver and gall bladder considerably disrupt these vital processes and can be held responsible to a large extend for the malfunctioning of any part of the body that depends for its health on the basic nutrients made available through the digestive system. The removal of all gallstones helps to normalise the digestive and eliminative functions, improve cell metabolism and maintain balance throughout the body.

Disorders of the Circulatory System

The *circulatory system* is divided for description into two main parts, the *blood circulatory system* and the *lymphatic system*. The *blood circulatory system* consists of the heart, which acts as a pump, and the blood vessels through which the blood circulates. The *lymphatic system* consists of lymph nodes and lymph vessels through which colourless *lymph* flows. The two systems work closely together and are intimately associated.

Heart Disease

The condition of the liver affects the entire circulatory system, including the heart. Normally, the liver detoxifies and purifies the venous blood that comes from the abdominal part of the digestive system, the spleen and the pancreas via the *portal vein*. Apart from breaking down alcohol the liver detoxifies noxious substances such as toxins produced by microbes, kills bacteria and parasites, and neutralises certain drug compounds through enzymes. It removes the nitrogenous portion from the amino acids, not required for the formation of new protein, and forms *urea* from this waste product, which is excreted in urine. It also breaks down the nucleoprotein of worn-out cells of the body to form uric acid and excretes it with urine.

The liver filters more than a quart of blood each minute, leaving only the acidic carbon dioxide for elimination through the lungs. After being purified in the liver the blood passes through the *hepatic vein* into the *inferior vena cava* which takes it to the right side of the heart. From there the venous blood is carried to the lungs where the interchange of gases takes place: carbon dioxide is excreted and oxygen absorbed. The oxygenated blood then passes into the left side of the heart from where it is pumped into the aorta, which supplies all body tissues.

Gallstones in the *bile* ducts of the liver distort the basic framework of the *lobules* and cause the blood vessels to develop kinks, which reduces internal blood supply. Liver cells become damaged and toxic cell debris enters the blood stream. The *detox capacity* of the liver becomes impaired and increasing amounts of harmful substances are retained, which further overtaxes liver functions.

In addition, cell protein and unused food proteins are not sufficiently broken down which raises the protein concentration in the blood. The number of red blood cells begins to rise which raises the packed cell volume of the blood called **Haemocrit** to abnormal levels. The concentration of **Haemoglobin** in the red blood cells also begins to increase, giving rise to a red complexion of the skin, particularly in the face and chest. (*Haemoglobin* is a complex protein that combines with oxygen in the lungs and transports it to all body cells.) Consequently, the red blood cells enlarge and become too big to pass through the tiny channels of the capillary network. The blood as a whole becomes thick and has a tendency to clot, which is considered the major risk factor for suffering a **heart attack** or a **stroke**. Since fat has no clotting ability, this risk stems mainly from the high concentration of protein in the blood. To continue distributing important nutrients, especially water, to the cells and eliminating their metabolic waste products, the body may have to raise the blood pressure. This natural response to an unnatural situation, however, unduly stresses and damages the blood vessels.

To avoid a heart attack, the capillaries absorb excessive protein, rebuild it into *collagen* and store it in their *basement membranes*. This thins the blood again but leads to thickening and subsequent damage of the blood vessel walls. Since the cells in the body no longer receive adequate amounts of oxygen, *haemoglobin* concentrations in the blood begin to rise further and the blood thickens once more. When the capillaries' storage capacity for protein is exhausted the *basement membranes* of the arteries also begin to absorb protein. Finally, cholesterol and other substances in the blood begin to attach themselves to the damaged sites, which has occluding effects. The gradual destruction of blood vessels is known as **arteriosclerosis**.

High Cholesterol

Cholesterol is an essential building block of all our body cells and is needed for every metabolic process. Normally, our body produces about half a gram to one gram of cholesterol a day depending on how much the body requires at the time.

Overall, our body can produce 400 times more cholesterol a day than what we would obtain from eating 100g butter. The main cholesterol producers are the liver and the small intestines; they release the cholesterol into the blood stream where it is instantly tied to blood proteins that are in charge of transporting it to their destinations. These proteins are called 'Lipo Proteins.' There are three types of lipoproteins in charge of transporting cholesterol: *The Low Density Lipoprotein* (LDL), the *Very Low Density Lipoprotein* (VLDL) and *the High Density Lipoprotein* (HDL).

LDL and VLDL are relatively large cholesterol molecules when compared to HDL. Yet due to the unique grid-like structure of the *sinusoids* they are able to leave the blood stream in the liver and reach the liver cells where they are rebuilt and then excreted with *bile* into the intestines. Once they enter the intestines they combine with fats and enter the blood. Gallstones in the *bile* ducts of the liver inhibit the *bile* flow and partially block their escape route. Due to backpressure on the liver, *bile* production drops. Normally the liver produces over a quart of *bile* a day. When the major *bile* ducts are blocked, barely a cup or even less will find its way to the intestines. This prevents much of the VLDL and LDL cholesterol from being excreted with the *bile*.

Gallstones in the liver bile ducts distort the structural framework of the liver *lobules,* which damages and congests the *sinusoids*. Whereas the good cholesterol HLD has small enough molecules to leave the blood stream through ordinary capillaries, the larger LDL and VLDL molecules are trapped. The result is that LDL and VLDL concentrations (considered to be the bad cholesterol) begin to rise in the blood to levels that are harmful for the body. In addition to this complication, reduced *bile* flow impairs the digestion of food, particularly fats, and therefore not enough cholesterol is available for the cells of the body and their basic metabolic processes. Since the liver cells no longer receive enough of the LDL and VLDL molecules they assume that the blood does not have enough of them. This stimulates the liver cells to increase the production of cholesterol, further raising the levels of LDL and VLDL cholesterol in the blood.

The bad cholesterol is trapped in the circulatory system

because its escape routes, the *bile* ducts and the liver *sinusoids*, are blocked or damaged. The capillary network and arteries absorb as much of the bad cholesterol as they possibly can, mixing it with the stored proteins. Consequently, the arteries begin to become hard and rigid.

Coronary heart disease, whether it is caused by smoking, drinking excessive amounts of alcohol, overeating protein foods, stress or any other factor never occurs unless gallstones have impacted the bile ducts of the liver first. Removing gallstones from the liver and gall bladder prevents heart attacks and strokes and reverses coronary heart disease. The body's response to stressful situations becomes less damaging and cholesterol levels normalise as the distorted and damaged liver *lobules* are regenerated. The theory of high cholesterol being a principal cause of coronary heart disease is unproved and unscientific. *Cholesterol* is not a *cause* of heart disease; it is an *effect* of a dysfunctional liver and circulatory system. By treating the cause or causes of elevated cholesterol, as a natural consequence, heart functions will return to normal.

Poor Circulation, Enlargement of Heart and Spleen, Varicose Veins, Hormonal Imbalances

Gallstones in the liver may lead to poor circulation, enlargement of heart and spleen and varicose veins. When gallstones have grown large enough to distort the structural framework of the lobules of the liver, the flow of blood through the liver becomes impeded. This not only raises the venous pressure in the liver but also in all the organs and areas of the body that drain their blood through their respective veins into the portal vein of the liver. The congestion in the portal vein of the liver causes congestion particularly in the spleen, stomach, distal end of the oesophagus, pancreas, gall bladder, small and large intestines. This can cause enlargement any or all of these organs, reduce their ability to remove cell waste products, and congest their respective veins.

A varicose vein is one, which is so dilated that the valves do not close to prevent blood from flowing backward. Sustained pressure on the veins at the junction of the rectum and anus in the large intestine leads to the development of *haemorrhoids*. Other common sites of varicose veins are the legs, the oesophagus and the scrotum. Dilation of veins and venules (small veins) can occur anywhere in the body. It always indicates an obstruction of blood flow.[1]

Poor blood flow through the liver also affects the heart. When the above organs of the digestive system become weakened by an increase in venous pressure, they become congested and b[2]egin to accumulate toxic waste, including debris that arises from decaying cell material. The spleen becomes enlarged to deal with the extra workload associated with removing damaged or worn out blood cells. This further reduces blood circulation to and from the organs of the digestive system, which **stresses the heart**, **raises blood pressure** as well as hardens and **injures blood vessels**. The right side of the heart, which receives venous blood from the liver and all other parts below the lungs through the *inferior vena cava*, becomes overloaded with toxic, sometimes infectious material, which causes enlargement.

Most types of heart disease have one thing in common: there is an obstruction of blood flow. The most severe obstructions with the most serious consequences for the circulatory system occur in the liver. The obstructions are gallstones impacting the bile ducts and cutting off the blood supply to the liver cells. Reduced blood flow through the liver always affects the blood flow in the entire body, which in turn has a detrimental effect on the lymphatic system.

The lymphatic system, which can be considered to be an important part of the immune system, helps to clear the body of

[1] Prescribed by doctors in Germany as a highly successful alternative to surgery for varicose veins, the herbal remedy horse chestnut seeds, or conkers is also effective in the treatment of heavy legs, haemorrhoids, and cramps. In combination with cleansing of the liver, colon, and kidneys, conkers can lead to complete recovery.

foreign matter and cell debris. All cells release metabolic waste products into and take up nutrients from a surrounding fluid called *extracellular fluid* or *connective tissue*. The degree of nourishment and efficiency of the cells depends on how swiftly and completely the waste material is removed from this fluid. Since some of the waste products cannot pass directly into the blood for excretion, they accumulate in the extracellular fluid until they are removed and detoxified by the lymphatic system. The main function of the lymphatic system consists of keeping the extracellular fluid of tissue clear of toxic substances, which makes this system to be one of utmost importance.

Poor circulation of blood in the body causes an overload of foreign, harmful matter in the extracellular tissues and consequently in the lymph vessels and the lymph nodes. The thymus gland, tonsils, and spleen, which are an important part of this cleansing system in the body, deteriorate fast if lymph flow becomes impaired. Also microbes harboured in gallstones can be a constant source of infection in the body which may render the lymphatic system ineffective against the more serious infections such as **infectious mononucleosis, measles, typhoid fever, tuberculosis, syphilis,** etc.

Due to restricted bile flow from the liver and gall bladder, the small intestine is restricted in its capacity to digest food, which permits unduly large amounts of metabolic waste and poisonous substances such as *cadaverines* and *putrescines* (resulting from fermented and putrefied food) to seep into the blood and lymph channels. Toxins (and also nutrients) enter the major lymph duct (thoracic duct) at the *cisterna chyli* (the Latin name is 'Radix') -- a lymph dilation situated in front of the bodies of the first two lumbar vertebrae. Due to the toxins as well as microbial activity and allergic reactions to food particles, the 'Radix' becomes inflamed and begins to swell. There is a **lymphoedema**, which can be felt as a hard knot as large as the size of a fist in the area of the navel. This "rock" is a major cause of **low back pain** and **abdominal swelling**.

Eighty percent of the lymphatic system is associated with the intestines, making this area of the body to be the largest centre of immune activity. This is no coincidence. The part in the body

24

where most disease-causing agents are or can be generated is the intestinal tract. Any lymphatic obstruction or a *lymphoedema* in this important part of the lymphatic system can lead to further lymphatic obstructions elsewhere in the body. Whenever a lymph vessel is obstructed, there is an accumulation of lymph distal to the obstruction. Consequently, the lymph nodes can no longer adequately deal with dead and live phagocytes and their ingested microbes, with worn-out tissue cells, with cells damaged by disease, with products of fermentation, pesticides in the food, inhaled or congested toxic particles and cells from malignant tumours. This may cause them to become inflamed, enlarged and congested with blood. Infected material may enter the blood, causing septic poisoning and acute diseases.

Lymphatic obstruction can also give rise to serious, chronic complications. For example, if it occurs in the *thoracic duct,* as it is with most illnesses, the retained debris may cause the development of the following ailments: ***cysts in the uterus or ovaries, enlargement of the prostrate gland, rheumatism in the joints, enlargement of the heart and congestive heart failure, congested bronchi and lungs, stiff neck, headaches, migraines, dizziness, vertigo, ringing in the ears, dandruff, colds, heyfever, certain types of asthma, thyroid enlargement, sinusitis, earaches, deafness, diseases of eyes, poor vision, swelling in the breasts, kidney problems, lower back pains, swelling of legs and ankles, scoliosis, etc.***

In addition to blocking proper lymph drainage from these various organs and parts of the body, congestion in the *thoracic duct* permits toxic materials to be released into the blood at the left *subclavian vein* in the root of the neck. This vein enters the *superior vena cava*, which leads straight into the right side of the heart. Some of the toxins may be deposited in the heart and heart arteries leading to heart disease and others may re-enter the general circulation spreading disease-causing agents into all parts of the body. In fact, there is rarely a disease that is not directly caused by lymphatic obstruction which in turn finds its origin in a congested liver (the causes of gallstones in the liver are being discussed in the following chapter). In the extreme eventuality, **cancer of the lymph** or *lymphoma* may result, of which **Hodgkin's disease** is the most common one.

When the circulatory system becomes affected as a result of gallstones in the liver, the entire *endocrine system* begins to malfunction. The endocrine glands produce hormones that pass directly from the cells (of the glands) into the blood stream. The body to influence activity, growth and nutrition uses hormones. The glands most often affected by congestion of lymph and blood are the thyroid, parathyroid, adrenal cortex, ovaries, and testes. Severe disruption of circulation causes imbalanced hormone secretions in the *Islets of Langerhans* in the Pancreas, pineal and pituitary.

Blood and lymph congestion, which is characterised by thickening of blood, makes it difficult for hormones to reach their target places in the body on time. Consequently the glands go into *hypersecretion* (overproduction) of hormones. When lymph drainage from the glands is inadequate the glands themselves become congested which may lead to *hyposecretion* (lack) of the corresponding hormones. Diseases related to imbalances of the thyroid glands include **toxic goitre, graves disease, cretinism, myxoedema, tumours of the thyroid, hypoparathyroidism** which reduces calcium absorption and causes **cataracts** as well as behavioural disturbances and **dementia**.

If circulatory problems interfere with insulin activity of the pancreatic *islets of Langerhans*, **diabetes** results. Gallstones in the liver can lead to diminished protein synthesis, which in turn prompts the adrenal glands to overproduce *cortisol*, which is a hormone that stimulates protein synthesis. Too much *cortisol* in the blood also gives rise to **atrophy of lymphoid tissue** and a **depressed immune response**, which is a leading cause of cancer and many other major illnesses. An imbalance in the secretion of adrenal hormones can cause almost every type of disorder as it leads to diminished **febrile response** and **diminished protein synthesis**. Proteins are the major building blocks for tissue cells, hormones, etc. The liver itself produces many different hormones, which affects the way the body grows and heals. It also inactivates hormones, *including insulin, glucagon, cortisol, aldosterone, thyroid and sex hormones*. Gallstones in the liver impair this vital function. This may increase hormone concentrations in the blood. Hormone imbalance is a very serious condition and can easily occur when gallstones in the liver have disrupted major circulatory pathways that are also hormonal pathways.

Disease is absent when blood and lymph flow is unhindered and normal. Both, circulatory and lymphatic problems can successfully be eliminated through a series of liver cleanses and be prevented by following a balanced diet and lifestyle.

Disorders of the Respiratory System

The body's health depends on the effectiveness and vitality of its cells. Most of the energy required by the cells is derived from chemical reactions that can only take place in the presence of oxygen. The resulting waste product is carbon dioxide. The respiratory system provides the route by which sufficient oxygen is taken into the body and it provides the route of excretion of carbon dioxide. Blood serves as a transport system for these gases between the lungs and the cells.

Gallstones in the liver can impair respiratory functions and cause **allergies, disorders of the nose, nasal cavities** and **diseases of the bronchi and lungs.** When gallstones distort the lobules of the liver, the blood-cleansing ability of the liver, small intestine, and lymphatic system becomes impaired. Waste material and other toxic substances, normally rendered harmless, have the opportunity to enter the heart, lungs, bronchi, and other respiratory passages. Constant exposure to these agents breaks down the resistance of the respiratory system against them. Lymph congestion in the abdominal region reduces lymphatic drainage from the respiratory organs. **Pneumonia** results when protective processes fail to prevent inhaled or blood-borne microbes reaching and *colonising* the lungs.

In addition, gallstones harbour harmful microbes as well highly toxic and irritating material, which enter the blood via the damaged liver sites. Thus, gallstones are a constant source of immune suppression, which leaves the body and particularly the upper respiratory tract highly susceptible to both internal and external disease-causing factors. These include both blood-borne and air-borne microbes, cigarette smoke, alcohol, X-rays, corticosteroids, allergens, etc.

Further complications arise when enough gallstones have accumulated in the liver bile ducts to cause an enlargement of the liver. (Comment: Most people in the Western Hemisphere have an enlarged liver because it harbours large amounts of gallstones. What is generally considered to be a 'normal-sized' liver is far too large which can easily be seen by the handful of stones removed through the liver cleanse. The liver returns to its normal size within 6 months after the 5th or 6th cleanse).

The liver, situated in the upper abdominal cavity, spans almost the entire width of the body. Its upper and anterior surfaces are smooth and curved to fit under the surface of the diaphragm. When enlarged, the liver obstructs the movement of the diaphragm and prevents the lungs from extending to their normal capacity during inhalation. By contrast, a healthy liver permits the lungs to extend into the abdominal region, which puts pressure on the abdomen. Consequently, the abdomen moves forward as can be seen especially in healthy babies and in healthy adults. Due to the increased expansion of the abdomen during inhalation, blood and lymph are pressed upwards towards the heart which helps maintain proper circulation. An enlarged liver prevents full extension of the diaphragm and lungs, which causes reduced exchange of gases in the lungs, lymphatic congestion, and retention of excessive amounts of carbon dioxide in the lungs. The restricted intake of oxygen affects cellular functions throughout the body.

All diseases of the lungs, bronchi and upper respiratory passages are either caused or worsened by gallstones in the liver and can be improved or cured by eliminating them through the liver cleanse.

Disorders of the Urinary System

The urinary system is a very important excretory system of the body. It consists of two kidneys which form and excrete urine; two ureters which convey the urine from the kidneys to the urinary bladder; a urinary bladder where urine collects and is temporarily stored; a urethra through which urine is discharged from the urinary bladder to the exterior of the body. Smooth functioning of the urinary system is essential for maintaining the appropriate balance between water and substances dissolved in it, and between acid and alkalis. This system is also involved in the disposal of waste products resulting, for example, from the breakdown (catabolism) of cell protein in the liver.

Most diseases of the kidneys and other parts of the urinary system are related to an imbalance of *simple filtration* in the kidneys. About 100 to 150 litres of dilute filtrate are formed each day by the two kidneys. Of these 1 to 1,5 litres are excreted as urine. With the exception of blood cells, platelets and blood proteins all other blood constituents pass through the kidneys. The process of filtration is greatly impaired by a weak performance of the digestive system and particularly by the liver.

Gallstones in the liver and gall bladder reduce the amount of bile necessary to digest food properly. Much of the undigested food begins to ferment and putrefy leaving toxic waste material in the blood and lymph. The waste products that cause disease are not the normal excretions of the body as the ones found in urine, sweat, gases, and faeces but tiny molecules that can only be made visible through the electro-microscope.

These molecules have a strong acidifying influence on the blood. To avoid a life-threatening disease or a coma, the blood must rid itself of these minute toxins. Hence they are deposited in the connective tissues of the organs. The connective tissue is a gel-like fluid that surrounds the cells, or you may say the cells are floating in the connective tissue. Normally, the body deals with acidic waste material that has been deposited there by releasing an alkaline product ($NaHCO_3$) into the blood that can retrieve and neutralise the toxins and eliminate them through the excretory organs. This emergency system, however, begins to fail when toxins are deposited faster than can be retrieved and eliminated. Consequently, the connective tissue may become as thick as jelly; nutrients, water and oxygen can not pass freely and the cells of the organs begin to suffer malnutrition, dehydration, and oxygen deficiency.

Gallstones particularly impair the liver's capacity to break down proteins from animal foods. Excessive proteins are temporarily stored in the connective tissues and then absorbed by the basement membranes of the capillaries. The basement membranes may become 10 times as thick as normal, which means that fewer toxins are able to escape the blood stream. This thickens the blood and makes it increasingly difficult for the kidneys to filter it. At the same time, the basement membranes of the blood vessels supplying the kidneys also become thickened. As this process of hardening of the arteries progresses further, blood pressure rises and overall kidney performance drops. Large amounts of metabolic waste from kidney cells, normally excreted through venous blood vessels and lymphatic ducts, are retained and further increase thickness of the cell membranes.

Hence the kidneys become overtaxed and are unable to maintain normal fluid and electrolyte balance. There may be precipitation of urinary components that form into crystals and stones of various types and sizes. **Uric acid stones** for example are formed when uric acid concentration in the urine exceeds the level of 2-4 mg %. This amount was still considered within the range of tolerance until the mid-sixties. Uric acid is a by-product of breaking down protein in the liver. Since meat consumption rose sharply at this time the maximum normal 'level' has been raised to 7,5 mg %. Yet this does not make uric acid less dangerous for the body. Uric acid stones can lead to **kidney urinary obstruction**, infection and even **kidney failure**. Malignant tumours may develop, as the cells become increasingly isolated and deprived of vital nutrients. An addition, uric acid crystals not eliminated by the kidneys can settle in the joints and cause rheumatism, gout and water retention.

All diseases of the urinary system are caused by toxic blood, i.e. blood saturated with tiny molecules of waste material and excessive proteins. Gallstones in the liver impair digestion, cause blood and lymph congestion and disrupt the entire circulatory system, including that of the urinary system. By removing the gallstones, the urinary system has a chance to recuperate, rid itself of existing accumulated toxins, stones, etc., and maintain fluid balance and normal blood pressure for all the processes in the body to take place smoothly and efficiently (also see 'The Kidney Cleanse' in "The Key to Health and Rejuvenation").

Disorders of the Nervous System

The nervous system, which includes the brain, the spinal cord, pairs of spinal and cranial nerves and an autonomic part, is largely dependent on the quality of the blood. Blood is composed of plasma, a straw-coloured transparent fluid, and cells. The constituents of plasma are water, plasma proteins, mineral salts, hormones, nutrient materials, organic waste products, antibodies and gases. There are three varieties of blood cells: White cells (leukocytes), red cells, (erythrocytes) and platelets (thrombocytes). Any abnormal changes in the blood affect the nervous system.

All three blood cell types are formed in the red bone marrow, which is nourished and maintained by the nutrients supplied through the digestive system. Gallstones in the liver greatly impair digestion and assimilation of food, which fills the plasma with excessive waste material and cuts down nutrient supplies to the red bone marrow. This in turn causes an imbalance in the constituents of the blood cells, disrupts hormonal pathways, and causes abnormal responses in the nervous system. Most diseases afflicting the nervous system are rooted in improperly formed blood caused by a dysfunctional liver.

All the functions of the liver directly influence the nervous system and particularly the brain. The liver cells convert glycogen (complex sugar) into glucose, which besides oxygen and water is the major nutrient for the nervous system. Glucose provides most of its energy requirements. The brain, although it constitutes only one fiftieth of the body weight, contains about one fifth of the total blood volume in the body. It uses up vast amounts of glucose. Gallstones in the liver drastically cut down glucose supply to the brain and the rest of the nervous system, which can affect the performance of each organ, the senses, and the mind. At this point, a person may develop food cravings, particularly for sweet or starchy foods, and may experience frequent mood swings or emotional stress.

The liver also forms the plasma proteins and most of the blood clotting factors from the available amino acids. This function becomes increasingly subdued by the presence of gallstones. If the production of clotting factors drops, platelet count will fall and there may be spontaneous capillary bleeding or *haemorrhagic disease*. If a haemorrhage occurs in the brain, this may cause destruction of brain tissue, paralysis, or death, depending on the severity of the condition and its possible triggers such as hypertension, alcohol abuse, etc. Platelet counts also decrease when production of new cells does not keep pace with destruction of damaged or worn out cells, as it happens for example in the liver when gallstones cut off blood supply to liver cells.

Vitamin K is also essential for synthesis of major clotting factors. It is a fat-soluble vitamin stored in the liver and bile salts are required in the colon for absorption. Vitamin K becomes deficient when gallstones in the liver and gall bladder obstruct bile flow, which leads to inadequate fat absorption.

As discussed earlier, gallstones in the liver can lead to disorders of the vascular system. When the blood changes and becomes thick, blood vessels begin to harden and become damaged. If a blood clot forms in an injured artery, a piece of blood clot (*embolus*) may lodge in a small artery distal to the injury and obstruct the blood flow, causing **ischaemia** and **infarction**. If the infarction occurs in a brain artery, it is called a **stroke**.

All circulatory disturbances affect the brain and the rest of the nervous system. The disruption of liver functions particularly affect atrocytes - cells that form the main supporting tissue of the central nervous system. The condition is characterised by apathy, disorientation, delirium, muscular rigidity, and coma. Nitrogenous bacterial waste absorbed from the colon, normally detoxified by the liver, reaches the brain cells via the blood. Other metabolic waste products such as ammonia may reach toxic concentrations and change the permeability of the blood vessels in the brain and reduce the effectiveness of the blood-brain barrier. This may permit other noxious substances to enter the brain as well, causing further damage.

If the neurones of the brain no longer receive enough nourishment, there is atrophy of neural tissue, which leads to *dementia* or *Alzheimer's disease*. In case the neurones responsible for producing the brain hormone and neuro-transmitter *dopamine* suffer malnutrition, *Parkinson's disease* results. *Multiple Sclerosis (MS)* occurs when the cells that produce *myelin*, a sheath of fatty material, which surrounds most axons of nerve cells, suffer malnutrition, and the myelin sheath diminishes and axons become injured.

The liver controls the digestion, absorption and metabolism of fatty substances throughout the body. Gallstones interfere with fat metabolism and affect cholesterol levels in the blood. *Cholesterol* is an essential building block of all our body cells and is needed for every metabolic process. Our brain consists of more than 10% pure cholesterol (all water removed). It is important for brain development and brain function. Cholesterol protects the nerves against damage or injury; any imbalance of blood fats can cause disruption of the nervous system and therefore lead to almost any type of disease in the body. Removing all gallstones from the liver and gall bladder increases nutrient supplies to all the cells, thereby rejuvenating the nervous system and improving all the functions in the body.

Disorders of the Bone

Although bone is the hardest tissue in the body, it is nevertheless very much alive. Human bone consists of 20%

water, 30-40% organic material such as living cells and 40-50% inorganic material such as calcium. Bone tissue also harbours many blood and lymph vessels and nerves. The bone cells responsible for bone formation are the *osteoblasts* and *osteoclasts*. *Osteoblasts* are the bone forming cells and *osteoclasts* are responsible for resorption of bone to maintain optimum shape. A third group of cells known as *chondrocytes* form cartilage. Red bone marrow, which forms red and white blood cells, is always present in the less dense parts of the bone called *cancellous bone*.

Most bone diseases occur when bone cells no longer receive enough nourishment through the lymph. Gallstones in the liver always lead to lymph congestion in the intestinal tract and consequently in other parts of the body (see "Disorders of the Circulatory System"). Normal bone is maintained through the fine balance of *osteoblast* and *osteoclast* activity. This balance is disturbed when deficient nutrient supply slows the production of new bone by the *osteoblasts*. Osteoporosis results when the amount of bone tissue is reduced because its deposition does not keep pace with resorption. *Cancellous bone* is usually affected before *compact bone*, which is the outer layer of the bone.

In generalised osteoporosis excess calcium is resorbed from bone and raises the blood and urine calcium levels, predisposing to stone formation in the kidneys which may lead to renal failure. Gallstones in the liver drastically cut down the production of bile, which is essential for the absorption of calcium from the small intestines. Even if food contains sufficient calcium or extra calcium is supplied through supplementation, the lack of bile makes much of the ingested calcium useless for bone formation and other important metabolic processes. In addition, the presence of gallstones in the liver raises the level of toxic acids in the blood, part of which are neutralised by calcium released by bones and teeth. Eventually, these reservoirs of calcium become depleted reducing bone density or bone mass. This may lead to bone and hip fractures and even death.

Rickets and *Osteomalacia* are diseases that affect the calcification process of bones. The bones remain soft and particularly those of the lower limbs become *bowed* by the weight of the body. Insufficient bile secretion and disturbance of the cholesterol metabolism, both caused by gallstones in the liver, as well as lack of exposure to ultraviolet light, reduces the fat-soluble vitamin D or Calciferol which is essential for calcium and phosphorus metabolism.

Infection of bones or *osteomyelitis* may result when there has been a prolonged lymphatic obstruction in the body and particularly in the bones and blood-borne microbes gain unchecked access to bones. The microbes may originate from gallstones, a tooth abscess or a boil.

Malignant tumours of the bone can occur when lymphatic congestion in the body and in the bones has reached extreme proportions. The immune system is depressed and malignant tumour particles from the breasts, lungs, or prostrate gland spread to bones that have the best blood supply, i.e. the *cancellous* bone. Bone cancer and all other diseases of the bone signify lack of nourishment of bone tissue and can rarely be improved unless all gallstones in the liver are removed and all other organs of elimination are cleansed as well.

3. **Disorders of the Joints**

There are three types of joints in our body: *Fibrous* or fixed joints, *cartilaginous* or slightly movable joints and *synovial* or freely movable joints. The most susceptible to disease are the joints of the hands, feet, knees, shoulders, elbows, and hips. The most commonly found diseases include *rheumatoid arthritis*, *osteoarthritis* and *gout*.

Most people with *rheumatoid arthritis* have a long history of intestinal complaints, bloatedness, wind, heartburn, belching, constipation, diarrhoea, coldness and swelling of hands and feet, increased perspiration, general fatigue, loss of appetite, weight reduction, etc. It is very likely then to conclude that *rheumatoid* arthritis is linked with any of these symptoms of major intestinal and metabolic disorders.

The gastrointestinal tract is constantly exposed to a large

number of viruses, bacteria, and parasites. In addition to the masses of antigens (foreign material) contained in the food and their break down products, the digestive system also has to deal with insecticides, pesticides, hormones, antibiotic residues, preservatives and colourings that are contained in so many foodstuffs today. Other antigens include pollen from flowers, plants, plant antibodies, fungi, bacteria, and some large molecule drugs such as penicillin. It is the task of the immune system, most part of which is located in the intestinal wall, to protect us against all of these potentially harmful invaders and substances. To be able to accomplish this task on a daily basis, both the digestive and lymphatic systems most be unobstructed and efficient. Gallstones in the liver severely disrupt the digestive process, which leads to an overload of the above toxic substances in the blood and lymph (see "Disorders of the Circulatory System).

Arthritis is an *autoimmune disease* affecting *synovial* membrane. Autoimmunity (the immune system develops immunity to its own cells) results when antigen/antibody complexes (*rheumatoid factors*) are formed and are present in the blood. Naturally, the B-lymphocytes (immune cells) in the intestinal wall become stimulated and produce antibodies (*immunoglobulins*) when coming into contact with above antigens. The immune cells circulate in the blood and some settle in the lymph nodes, the spleen, the mucus membrane of the salivary glands, the lymphatic system of the bronchial tubes, the vagina or uterus, the milk-producing mammary glands of the breasts and in the capsular tissues of the joints.

If there is repeated exposure to the same types of toxic antigens, resulting, for example, from fermenting and putrefying food (and accompanying intense microbial activity), antibody production will increase dramatically, particularly in areas where immune cells have settled due to a previous encounter with the invaders. This will raise the level of antigen/antibody complexes in the blood and upset the fine balance that exists between the immune reaction and its suppression. *Autoimmune diseases*, which indicate an extremely high level of toxicity in the body, directly result from a disturbance of this balance. If antibody production is continually high in *synovial joints*, inflammation becomes chronic, leading to increasing deformity, pain and loss of function. The overuse of the immune system leads to *self-destruction* in the body. If this form self-destruction occurs in nerve tissue it is called MS, and if it occurs in organ tissue, it is called cancer.

Osteoarthritis is a degenerative non-inflammatory disease. It occurs when the renewal of *articular cartilage* (a smooth, strong surface covering the bones in contact with other bones) does not keep pace with its removal. The *articular cartilage* gradually becomes thinner until eventually the bony articular surfaces come into contact and the bones begin to regenerate. Abnormal bone repair and chronic inflammation may follow this. This disease is caused by a long-standing digestive disorder. The nourishment of bone and articular cartilage becomes increasingly difficult as fewer nutrients are absorbed and distributed for tissue formation. Gallstones in the liver impair the basic digestive processes and therefore play perhaps the most important role in the development of *osteoarthritis*.

Gout is another joint disease directly connected to weak liver performance. Sodium urate crystals in joints and tendons cause it. *Gout* occurs in some people whose blood *uric acid* is abnormally high. When gallstones in the liver begin to affect blood circulation in the kidneys (see "Urinary Disorders"), *uric acid* excretion becomes defective. This also causes increased cell damage and cell destruction both in the liver and kidneys and also in other parts of the body. *Uric acid* is a waste product of the breakdown of cell nuclei and is produced in excess with increased cell destruction. Smoking cigarettes, drinking alcoholic beverages regularly, using stimulants, etc. cause marked cell destruction, which releases large quantities of cell protein into the blood stream. In addition, uric acid production rises sharply with over-consumption of protein foods such as meat, fish, eggs, cheese, etc. (also see 'The Kidney Cleanse' in *"The Key to Health and Rejuvenation"*). There may be several acute attacks of arthritis before the condition becomes chronic and damage of joints decreases mobility.

Disorders of the Reproductive Systems

Both, female and male reproductive systems largely depend on smooth functioning of the liver. Gallstones in the liver obstruct the movement of bile through the bile ducts, which impairs digestion and distorts the structural framework of liver lobules. This diminishes the liver's production of *serum albumin*, the most common abundant protein in the blood responsible for maintaining plasma osmotic pressure at its normal level of 25mmHg, and *clotting factors,* essential for coagulation of blood. Insufficient osmotic pressure cuts down the supply of nutrients to the cells, including those of the reproductive organs. This may lead to reduced lymph drainage and subsequently to fluid retention and oedema, as well as retention of metabolic waste and gradual impairment of sexual functions.

Most diseases of the reproductive system result from improper lymph drainage. The *thoracic duct* (see Disorders of the Circulatory System) which drains lymph from all organs of the digestive system, including the liver, spleen, pancreas, stomach and intestines becomes often severely congested when gallstones in the liver impair digestion and absorption of food. This also affects the organs of the reproductive system, which empty their lymph into the *thoracic duct.*

Impaired lymphatic drainage from the female pelvic area of the body is responsible for suppressed immunity, menstrual problems, PMT, menopausal symptoms, pelvic inflammatory disease (PID), cervicitis, all uterine diseases, vulvar dystrophies with growth of fibrous tissue, ovarian cysts and tumours, cell destruction, hormone deficiencies, low libido, infertility and genetic mutations of cells leading to cancer. Thoracic blockage may also lead to lymph congestion in the left breast leaving deposits of noxious substances which cause inflammation, form lumps and even tumours. If the right lymphatic duct, which drains lymph from the right half of the thorax, head and neck and the right arm becomes congested, toxins are retained in the right breast leading to similar problems there.

A continuous restriction of lymph drainage from the male pelvic area causes benign and malignant prostrate enlargement, inflammation of the testes, penis and urethra. Impotence is likely. The consistent increase of gallstones in the liver, a common factor among middle aged men in affluent societies, is one of the major reasons for lymph blockage in this vital part of the body. Even venereal diseases can only occur when there is a high level of toxicity in the exposed area due to lymph blockage, prior to microbial infection. The broken defence capacity of the lymphatic system against invading organisms causes most of the reproductive and sexual disorders. By removing all gallstones from the liver and taking recourse to a healthy diet and life-style, lymphatic activity can return to normal. Infections subside; cysts, fibrous tissue and tumours are broken down and removed; sexual functions are restored.

Disorders of the Skin

All skin diseases such as *eczema*, *acne*, and *psoriasis* have one factor in common: gallstones in the liver. Every person with a skin disease also has intestinal problems and impure blood in particular, mainly caused by gallstones. Since gallstones contribute to so many types of problems in the body - particularly those of the digestive system, the circulatory system and urinary system - the skin as a major organ of elimination becomes heavily overtaxed; it attempts to eliminate what the colon, kidneys, lungs and liver were unable to remove or detoxify. The toxic material is first deposited in the connective tissue under the *dermis*. When this 'waste depot' is saturated the skin begins to malfunction.

Excessive amounts of noxious substances, cell debris, microbes from various sources such as gallstones, and various antigens from improperly digested foods congest the lymphatic system and inhibit proper lymph drainage from the various layers of the skin. The toxins and putrefying protein from damaged or destroyed skin cells attract microbes and become a source for constant irritation and inflammation of the skin. Skin cells begin to suffer malnutrition, greatly reducing their turnover time. This may also cause extensive damage to the nerves.

If the sebaceous glands which pour their secretion, *sebum*, into the hair follicles, become nutrient deficient, hair growth becomes abnormal and particularly **scalp hair may fall out**. When *melanin* supply becomes deficient, the **hair turns grey**. *Sebum* deficiency also alters the healthy texture of the hair and makes it look dull and unattractive. On the skin *sebum* acts as a bactericidal and fungicidal agent, preventing the successful invasion of microbes. It also prevents drying and cracking of the skin, especially with exposure to sunshine and hot, dry air.

Genetic predisposition towards developing baldness or any other skin disorders is *not* a major causative factor as is often assumed. Healthy skin functions are restored and hair growth particularly among women is returned to normal once all gallstones are removed, the colon is cleansed and kidney/bladder functions improved (for details regarding colonic irrigation and kidney cleanse see *"The Key to Health and Rejuvenation"*).

Conclusion

Gallstones are a major cause of illness in the body. They impair the functioning of the most versatile and influential organ of the body – the liver. Nobody has ever devised an artificial liver because it is so complex. Second only to the brain in complexity, the liver masterminds the most intricate processes of digestion and metabolism, thereby affecting the life and health of every cell in the body. By removing the obstacles that prevent the liver from doing its job properly and efficiently, the body can return to a state of continuous balance.

Chapter 3

How do I Know I have Gallstones?

From my personal experiences with thousands of patients suffering from almost any kind of illness, including the so-called *terminal diseases*, each person had large numbers of gallstones in the liver and in many cases also in the gall bladder. By eliminating the stones through the liver cleanse and introducing simple health-forming habits and supportive measures, the patients have recovered from diseases that have defied both conventional and alternative methods of treatment.

The following are some signs and indications showing the presence of gallstones in the liver and gall bladder. If you have any of them you are most likely to derive great benefits from having a liver cleanse. In my practice I have found these indications to be highly accurate. In case you are not sure whether you have stones or not, it may be useful to do cleanse the liver anyway for it can improve your health significantly. The final proof lies with you. Only by doing the cleanse, you can prove to yourself that you had gallstones in the liver. You will also discover that by removing all the stones the symptoms of disease will gradually disappear and health return to normal.

Signs and Marks

The Skin

The skin's major function is to continuously adjust our internal body to the ever-changing external environment, i.e. temperature, humidity and dryness, light, etc., and to protect us

41

against injury, microbes and other harmful agents. But the skin also changes according to internal changes taking place within in the body and thus reflects the condition of the organs and body fluids such as the blood and lymph. Any long-term abnormal functioning of the body will show up in the skin as skin blemishes, discoloration, or changed condition such as dryness, oiliness, wrinkles, etc. All skin disorders have their root in an imbalanced liver condition. Gallstones lead to circulatory disorders, which reduces the nutrient supply to the skin and prevents healthy development and turnover of skin cells. The following marks are particularly indicative of gallstones in the liver and gall bladder.

Black spots, small or large brown patches that are of the colour of freckles, or *moles* appearing on the right or left side of the forehead, between the eyebrows, under the eyes, and just above the right shoulder or between the shoulder blades. Most prominent are the so-called *liver spots* on the back of the hands and forearms, often seen among middle aged and elderly people. If gallstones that were excreted by the gall bladder get caught in the colon such spots will appear in the area where thumb and index finger meet. The liver spots and marks begin to fade after all stones are removed from the liver and gall bladder.

Vertical wrinkles between the eyebrows. There may be one deep line or two, sometimes three lines in this region. These wrinkles, which are *not* a part of natural ageing, indicate an accumulation of many gallstones in the liver. The liver is expanded and has hardened. The deeper and longer the wrinkles are, the more progressed the deterioration of liver function is. The vertical lines also represent a great deal of repressed frustration and anger. Anger arises when gallstones prevent proper bile flow. If white or yellow patches accompany the wrinkles, there may be a cyst or tumour developing in the liver. Pimples or growth of hair between the eyebrows, with or without wrinkles, indicate that liver, gall bladder and spleen are affected.

Horizontal wrinkles across the bridge of the nose are a

sign of pancreatic disorders due to gallstones in the liver. If a line is very deep and pronounced, there may be *pancreatitis* or *diabetes.*

A green or dark colour of the temple area at the sides of the head show that the liver, gall bladder, pancreas and spleen are underactive due to the deposits of gallstones in both the liver and gall bladder. This may be accompanied by a green or blue colour on both sides of the bridge of the nose, which indicates impaired spleen functions.

An oily skin condition of the forehead also implies poor liver performance due to gallstones and so does *excessive perspiration* in this part of the head. *A yellow colour of the facial skin* indicates disorders of the bile functions of the liver and gall bladder, and a weakness of the pancreas, kidneys and excretory organs.

Hair loss in the central region of the head indicates that the liver, heart, small intestines, pancreas, and reproductive organs are becoming increasingly congested and rigid. There is a tendency to develop cardiovascular disease, chronic digestive problems, and formation of cysts and tumours. *Grey and white hair* shows that the liver and gall bladder functions are underactive.

The Nose

A nose that is hardening at the tip indicates chronic liver weakness resulting in a hardening of arteries and accumulation of fat around the heart, liver, spleen, kidneys, and prostate glands. If swelling or enlargement of the nose accompanies this condition, a heart attack or stroke may be imminent.

A red colour of the nose also shows an abnormal condition of the heart, with tendency towards hypertension. A purple nose indicates low blood pressure. Both conditions are caused by imbalanced liver functions.

A cleft nose or indentation of the tip of the nose indicates an irregular heartbeat and murmuring. If one half of the cleft part is larger than the other is, this shows that one side of the heart is abnormally enlarged. Arrhythmia and panic attacks may accompany this condition. There is severe lymphatic congestion caused by digestive disorders such as constipation, colitis, etc. The liver functions are suppressed because of large numbers of gallstones cutting off the blood supply to liver cells. Bile secretions are insufficient.

A nose bending towards the left indicates that the organs on the right hand side of the body - including the liver, gall bladder, right kidney, ascending colon, right ovary or testicle, are underactive. The main cause for this for this condition is an accumulation of gallstones in the liver and gall bladder (the nose will return to centre when the stones are removed).

The Eyes

A yellowish colour of the skin under the eyes indicates that the liver and gall bladder are overactive. A dark colour arises when the kidneys, bladder, and reproductive organs are overtaxed as a result of a long-standing disorder of the digestive functions. A greyish, pale colour occurs if the kidneys and sometimes the lungs are malfunctioning due to improper lymph drainage from these organs. Also the endocrine system may be affected.

Water or fat containing eyebags under the lower eyelid are due to congestion in the digestive and excretory organs caused by inadequate lymph drainage. If these eyebags are chronic, there is a tendency towards developing inflammation, cysts, and eventually tumours in the bladder, ovaries, Fallopian tubes, uterus, and prostate glands.

If a white cloud, consisting of mucous and protein particles, covers the pupil of the eye, it indicates that cataracts are developing.

Expanded capillaries, indicating disorders in the circulatory and respiratory functions cause a red colour in the white of the eye. White/yellow mucous patches show that the body is accumulating fatty substances; the liver and gall bladder functions are impaired. There is a tendency toward developing cysts, tumour and cancer.

A thick line of white colour covers parts of the periphery of the iris, particularly its lower parts. This is indicative of large amounts of cholesterol having accumulated in the circulatory and lymphatic system. (Note: if you wish to understand the connection of the eyes and iris to the various parts of the body, I recommend that you study the science of *iridology*, which is the diagnosis according to observation of the iris).

The Tongue, Mouth, Lips, and Teeth

The tongue is coated yellow/white, especially in its back part. This indicates an imbalance in the secretion of bile, which is the major cause of digestive trouble. Toxic residues of undigested, fermented or putrefied food lingers in the intestinal tract which congests the lymph in the thoracic duct and prevents toxins and microbes in the throat and mouth area from being removed.

There are teeth impressions on the sides of the tongue, often accompanied with white mucous discharge. This indicates weak digestion and inadequate absorption of nutrients from the small intestines.

Pimples on the tongue show weak digestion and presence of fermenting and putrefying food in the small and large intestines.

Cracks on the tongue are signs of an impaired colon

function. Food is not mixed sufficiently with bile and which permits toxic acids to injure and derange the colon walls. There may be little or no mucous discharge on the tongue.

Repeated mucous discharge into the throat and mouth. Bile may regurgitate into the stomach, which irritates its protective lining and causes excessive mucus production. Some of the bile and mucus may even move up towards the mouth. This may create a bad taste (bitter) in the mouth and give rise to frequent attempts of clearing the throat which at times involves coughing.

Poor breath and frequent burping indicates presence of undigested, fermenting or putrefying food in the gastrointestinal tract. Bacteria acting on the waste material produce gases, which can at times be very toxic, hence, the bad odour emanating from the breath.

The lips become dark in places when obstructions in the liver, gall bladder and kidneys have resulted in slowness and stagnation of blood circulation and lymph drainage throughout the body. There may be advanced abnormal constriction of blood capillaries. If the colour becomes reddish dark, heart, lungs and respiratory functions are subdued.

Crust formation at the corners of the mouth indicates the presence of duodenal ulcers caused by regurgitation of bile into the stomach. *Mouth ulcers* in various parts of the mouth or the tongue show that inflammation and ulceration occurs in the corresponding parts of the gastrointestinal tract. For example, a mouth ulcer on the inside or outside parts of your lower lip points at the presence small ulcer lesions in the large intestine. Herpes on the lip corresponds to more severe inflammation and ulceration of the intestinal wall.

Swollen or expanded lips indicate intestinal disorders. If the lower lip is swollen the colon suffers constipation, diarrhoea or both in alternation. Toxic gases are formed from improperly digested foods, which gives rise bloating and abdominal discomfort. A swollen or enlarged upper lip indicates stomach problems, including indigestion, frequently accompanied by "heartburn". An abnormal, tightly closed mouth shows that a person suffers from disorders of the liver, gall bladder, and possibly the kidneys. If the lower lip is dry, peels and splits easily, there may either be chronic constipation or diarrhoea and large amounts of toxins prevalent in the colon. This condition is accompanied by advanced dehydration of colon cells.

Swollen, sensitive or bleeding gums occur when lymph drainage from the mouth area is inefficient due to intestinal lymph congestion. There is an overload of acid compounds in the blood. Inflammation deep in the throat, with or without swelling of the tonsils is also caused by lymphatic blockage. *Tonsillitis*, which often occurs among children, is a sign of constant retention of toxins contained in the lymph.

Teeth problems in general are related to poor liver function. Tooth decay in particular is caused by nutritional imbalance. Poor digestion and overconsumption of refined, processed and highly acid forming foods such as sugar, chocolate, meat, cheese, coffee, soda, etc. deplete minerals and vitamins. Adults usually have 32 teeth. Each tooth corresponds to one of the 32 vertebrae of the spine and each vertebra is connected to a major organ or gland. If any of the 4 canines are decaying, it indicates the presence of large numbers of gallstones in the liver and gall bladder. A yellow colour of the teeth and the canines in particular may indicate disorders in all the mid-abdominal region, i.e. the liver, gall bladder, stomach, pancreas, spleen and their functions.

The Hands and Feet

White, fatty skin on the fingertips indicates disorders of the digestive and lymphatic systems and the liver and kidneys may be forming cysts and tumours. There is discharge of excessive fats and sugar.

Dark red fingernails show a high content of cholesterol, fatty acids, and minerals in the blood. The liver, gall bladder and spleen are congested and underactive and all excretory functions are overloaded. *Whitish nails* indicate accumulation of fat and mucus in and around the heart, the liver, pancreas, prostate and ovaries. This condition is accompanied by underactive blood circulation, and low haemoglobin—anaemia.

Vertical ridges on the nails generally indicate poor absorption of food and disruption of digestive, liver and kidney functions. *Strong vertical ridges on the thumbnails, possibly with split ends*, show that the functions of the testicles and ovaries are in disorder, caused by in an inefficient digestive and circularity system.

Hard protrusion at the ball of the foot. This condition shows progressive hardening of the organs in the middle of the body, including the liver, stomach, pancreas, and spleen. There are numerous gallstones in the liver and gall bladder. It also indicates physical and mental rigidity with a tendency toward domination, prejudice, and jealousy.

A yellow colour of the feet also indicates an accumulation of many stones in the liver and gall bladder. If the colour becomes green, spleen and lymph functions are severely disrupted which may lead to cysts, tumours and cancer.

Hardness at the tip of the fourth toe or a callous in the area under the fourth toe is an indication that gall bladder functions are stagnant. General rigidity, bent condition, and painful fourth toes show that there is a history of gallstones in the gall bladder and liver.

Curving of the first toe. If the large (first) toe curves abnormally, i.e. towards the second toe, it shows that the liver functions are subdued due to the presence of gallstones in the liver bile ducts. At the same time, spleen and lymphatic functions are overactive due to the accumulation of toxic residues from inadequately digested foods.

A white colour and rugged surfaces on the fourth and fifth toenails indicate disorders in the liver and gall bladder as well as the kidneys and bladder.

The Constitution of Faecal Matter

The stool or faecal matter emits sharp, sour or penetrative odour. This indicates that the food has not being digested properly. Fermented and putrefied food and presence of large amounts of harmful microbes in the faeces gives rises to its abnormal odour. This type of stool is generally not coated with a mucous lining, which normally prevents the anus from being soiled.

Dry and hard stools are an indication of constipation and so are sticky stools. Diarrhoea is yet another sign of weak performance of the digestive system and the liver in particular.

The faeces looks pale or clay-coloured, an indication of poor liver performance (bile gives the stool its natural brown colour). If it floats, large amounts of undigested fats are contained in it, which makes it lighter than water.

Conclusion: There may be many more signs and marks indicating the presence of gallstones in the liver and gall bladder than those listed above. Pain in the right shoulder, tennis elbow, frozen shoulder, numbness in the legs, sciatica, for example may have no obvious relation to gallstones that have accumulated in the liver, yet by removing the gallstones, these conditions disappear.

The body is a network of information and every part influences every other part. Seemingly insignificant marks or signs on the skin, in the eyes, or on a toe may be the harbingers of serious diseases. By recognising them and cleansing the liver and gall bladder and by taking recourse to a healthy regimen and life-style, signs and marks of wellness and vitality begin to dominate and replace the signs and marks of wellness and vitality. To prevent illness from arising and make health a permanent reality, it is necessary to understand what causes gallstones in the first place.

Chapter 4

The Most Common Causes of Gallstones

Bile consists of water, mucus, and bile pigment (bilirubin), bile salts, and cholesterol as well as enzymes and friendly, essential bacteria. This greenish fluid is produced by liver cells which pass it into tiny canals that join up to form larger canals until eventually they form the *right and left hepatic ducts* which drain bile from the liver. The two *hepatic ducts* join to form the *common bile duct* that supplies the gall bladder with the right amount of bile required for proper digestion of food.

Any changes in the composition of bile affect the solubility of its constituents and hence cause formation of gallstones. There are two types of gallstones, *cholesterol and pigment stones.* *Cholesterol stones* are composed of at least sixty- percent cholesterol; they have a pea green colour and are generally soft. *Pigment stones* are brown or black owing to their high content of coloured pigment (bilirubin). They may be calcified and are harder and more solid than the cholesterol stones. The latter can almost only be found in the gall bladder and are more prevalent among the Asian population.

Abnormal composition of bile can occur in a number of ways. Cholesterol is normally kept in liquid form by the dissolving action of bile salts (and of course the availability of sufficient amounts of water). An increased amount of cholesterol in the bile overwhelms the dissolving capacity of the bile salts, promoting the formation of cholesterol stones. Similarly, a decrease in the amount of bile salts also leads to cholesterol stone formation. If due to insufficient intake of water there is not

51

enough water to maintain the fluidity of bile, cholesterol cannot be dissolved properly and forms into small cholesterol pebbles.

Pigment stones form when bile pigment (bilirubin), a waste product of the breakdown of red blood cells increases in bile. Persons with excessive amounts of gallstones in the liver are at risk of developing liver cirrhosis, sickle-cell disease or other blood diseases which may increase presence of bilirubin pigment in bile, hence the formation of bilirubin stones in the gall bladder.

When the balanced composition of bile is disturbed in the liver, tiny cholesterol crystal begins to combine with other bile components and form tiny clots, which obstruct the tiny bile ducts known as *bile canaliculi*. This slows the bile flow further and more bile is added to the tiny clots, which eventually are large enough to be called gallstones. Some of these "grown" stones may pass into the larger bile ducts and combine there with other stones; hence the bile flow becomes obstructed there as well. If several of the larger bile ducts are congested, many hundreds of the smaller ones are then affected, leading to a vicious circle. Eventually, even the *hepatic ducts* clog up, drastically reducing the amount of bile available for the digestive process.

Sluggish bile flow in the liver alters the composition of bile even further, which subsequently affects the gall bladder. A small clot of bile in the gall bladder may take about 8 years to grow large enough to be noticeable and to become a serious health threat. It is known that one in ten Americans has gallstones in the gall bladder and that 500,000 opt for a gall bladder operation each year. What is not known, however, is that almost every person with any health problem has gallstones in the liver, which causes many more diseases than *just* stone formation in the gall bladder. To make a real and immediate breakthrough in the understanding and treatment of disease, we as individuals, need to understand what exactly dehydrates the bile fluid, alters its natural flora, destroys its enzymes, increases its cholesterol content, or changes the amount of bile pigment (bilirubin). The following four categories shed light on the most common factors responsible for causing gallstones.

1. <u>Dietary</u>

Overeating

Dietary mistakes play perhaps the biggest role in producing imbalanced bile compositions and consequently gallstones. Among all dietary mistakes, ***overeating*** is one of the worst. By regularly eating too much food or eating food more frequently than the body requires sustaining itself, the digestive juices, including bile, become increasingly depleted. This leaves large proportions of the ingested foods undigested and a source of harmful microbial activity. Large amounts of toxic substances begin to linger in the intestinal tract, congesting lymph and thickening the blood, overtaxing the liver and excretory functions.

Intestinal disorders can greatly deplete bile salts in the body, and lead to cholesterol gallstone formation. This is most notably evidenced by the increased risk of gallstones in patients with Crohn's disease, an inflammatory disease of bowel, and other forms of *Irritable Bowel Syndrome.*

An imbalanced blood and lymph condition caused by overeating leads to congestion of blood vessels in the liver, thereby altering bile composition and generating gallstones. Gallstones in the liver further congest blood and lymph, which upsets the body's basic metabolism. The more one overeats food, the fewer nutrients become available to the body cells. Constant overeating leads to starvation of the cells, which is expressed in the urge to eat food more often. The repeated desire to snack, known as food craving, is a sign of progressive malnutrition and metabolic imbalance. Moreover, it indicates an imbalanced liver activity and presence of gallstones.

Eating to the point that you feel full or cannot eat any more food is a situation where stomach functions are impaired altogether. Digestive juices in the stomach are only able to mix with the ingested food if the stomach is at least one quarter empty. Two cupped hands full of food equals about three-quarters of the size of your stomach which is the maximum amount the stomach can process at a time. It is best to stop eating at the point when you still could eat a little more. Leaving the dinner table slightly hungry helps improve the digestive functions and prevent gallstones and disease from arising in the future.

Eating in Between Meals

Ayurveda, the most ancient health science, considers *"eating before the previous meal has been digested"* to be one of the major causes of illness. A stressful and hurried life-style, the huge variety of processed, refined, and attractively packaged food stuff on offer, and the convenience of having fast food meals (low in nutritional value) may have contributed to the irregular eating habits prevalent in a large percentage of today's population. As a general rule, the more processed foods are, the less nutrients they contain, and the less nutrients they contain, the more of them we need to eat in order to satisfy the daily nutritional requirements of the body.

Irregular eating habits, which include eating in between meals, greatly upset the body's finely tuned biological rhythms that largely depend on regular cycles of eating, sleeping, and waking. The secretion of bile and intestinal digestive juices necessary for breaking down foods into their basic nutrient components is particularly high during midday which naturally asks for the biggest meal to be eaten during at around this time. In the morning and in the evening, the body's digestive capacity is considerably lower. If lunch consists only of a light snack, the gall bladder will not squeeze *all* its contents into the intestines, leaving behind enough bile to form gallstones. In addition, there will be a nutritional deficiency, which is expressed through a frequent desire to eat foods or have drinks that promise a quick boost in energy such as sweets, chocolates, coffee soda, etc. With every little snack, a little bile may be released by the gall bladder, which is not enough to empty it altogether, increasing further the risk of gallstone formation. To have the repeated desire to eat in between meals represents a major imbalance of the digestive and metabolic functions.

Each time you eat something, for example an hour or two after a meal the body is coerced to leave the previously eaten food half-digested and to attend the newly ingested food. The previous food begins to ferment and putrefy, becoming a source of toxins in the digestive tract, and the new food receives only inadequate amounts of digestive juices, leaving it half-digested as well. While being in the process of digesting food, the body is simply *not* capable of producing and delivering sufficient amounts of bile and other digestive juices for the newly arriving foods or drinks. This results in the generation of ever-increasing amounts of toxins and ever-decreasing amounts of nutrients. Both these stressful situations cause a reduction in bile salts and an increase of cholesterol production; hence the forming of gallstones.

To escape this vicious cycle, allow yourself to go through the initial phases of food cravings with more awareness and by substituting with fruit. In many people the urge to eat is often a sign of severe dehydration. Drinking 1-2 glasses of water can stop the discomfort altogether. At the same time, make certain that you get a substantial and nutritious meal at lunchtime. In time, and provided you have cleansed your liver, your body will receive enough nutrients from the main meal at lunchtime to satisfy all its daily nutritional requirements. This will effectively stop all food cravings and desires to eat in between meals.

Eating Large Meals in the Evenings

A similar situation occurs when the main meal of the day is consumed in the evening. Since the secretion of bile and digestive enzymes is drastically reduced after 6pm, a meal consisting for example of animal proteins such as meat, chicken, fish, cheese, oily or oil-fried foods, etc. will not be properly digested at this time. Instead it will become a source of toxic waste-deposits in the intestines.

Undigested foods are always a cause of congestion, first in

the intestines and then in the lymph and blood. This greatly affects the quality of digestion during daytime meals. Gradually, the digestive power, which is determined by the balanced secretion of hydrochloric acid, bile and digestive enzymes, becomes subdued causing the same side effects that arise from overeating. Thus, eating large meals in the evening is a principal source of gallstones in the liver. Eating food before going to sleep further upsets the digestive functions. Ideally, there should be at least three hours between eating and bedtime. The ideal time for dinner is around 6pm.

Excessive Protein Consumption

As discussed in the section "High Cholesterol," *Disorders of the Circulatory system,* excessive protein consumption leads to a thickening of the basement membranes of the blood vessels, including those of the liver *sinusoids*. Consequently, not enough *serum* cholesterol is able to leave the blood stream at the *sinusoids* and enter the liver cells, which must assume that there is a shortage of cholesterol in the body. This stimulates the liver cells to increase production of cholesterol to abnormally high levels. Hence bile which excretes cholesterol into the small intestines becomes too saturated with cholesterol, forming deposits of cholesterol in the liver bile ducts and later also in the gall bladder.

The book *"The Key to Health and Rejuvenation"* explains in greater detail how overconsumption of protein foods affects the circulatory system and that by reducing proteins in our diet, old deposits of protein in the basement membranes of the blood vessels can be removed again. Asians who generally have a low protein but fat-rich diet rarely have cholesterol stones in their gall bladders. On the other hand, cholesterol stones in the gall bladder are very common among Americans whose diet is rich in proteins.

Dietary fats play only an insignificant role in raising cholesterol levels in the blood. The body cells and particularly the cells of the liver produce most of the cholesterol we require on a daily basis for basic metabolic processes. It is the thickening of the basement membranes through protein deposits that raises cholesterol production in the liver to abnormal levels. In addition to eating protein foods, also smoking, drinking alcohol or coffee, and stress generate excessive amounts of proteins in the blood which when deposited in the blood vessel walls increases cholesterol production by the liver cells and promotes the formation of gallstones.

If you are not a vegetarian it is best to cut out meat, pork, and eggs and keep other types of animal protein to a minimum. Although all animal proteins have a gallstone- generating effect, white meat, including chicken, turkey, and rabbit, cause the least damage to the liver, provided they are of free-range origin and not eaten more often than once or twice a week. It is best to avoid fried foods as they aggravate both the gall bladder and liver. Once your taste for meat or other animal proteins begins to diminish, gradually switch to a balanced vegetarian diet. Vegetarians have the lowest incidence of gallstones, heart disease and cancer.

Specific Foods or Drinks

Eggs, pork, onions, fowl, pasteurised milk, coffee, citrus, corn, beans (except soy-beans), and nuts, in this order, are known to bring on gall bladder attacks in patients suffering from gall bladder disease. In a 1968 study (Ann Al, 1968, 26; 83-7) an entire group of patients with gall bladder disease were free of symptoms while on a diet free from above foods. Adding eggs to their diet brought on gall bladder attacks in 93% of patients. Egg proteins in particular can have a gallstone-producing effect. Researchers believe that the ingestion of substances which cause allergies make the bile ducts swell up, which in turn impairs the flow of bile from the gall bladder.

This however is only partially true. From Ayurveda's point of view gallstone formation is a so-called *Pitta* disorder, affecting mostly the *Pitta* body type. *Pitta,* which means bile in the language of *Sanskrit*, is naturally secreted in large amounts among this body-type but is also easily aggravated, that is its constituent parts become imbalanced when most of the above foods are eaten on a regular basis.

The *Pitta* body type is known to have only limited amounts of enzymes to break down the following foods or drinks of which the most prominent are: *Sour dairy products, including cheese, yoghurt, sour cream; egg yolks; salty butter; lentils; all nuts except almonds; hot spices, also ketchup, mustard, pickles, salt, sour salad dressings, spicy condiments, vinegar: citrus fruits and citrus fruit juices; all sour and unripe fruits; brown sugar; whole (non-ground) grains as contained in many whole wheat breads; brown rice; lentils; alcohol; tobacco, coffee and regular tea; most medical drugs; cokes and other soft drinks; artificial sweeteners, preservatives and colourings; chocolates, cacao; left-over or frozen foods; iced drinks.*

Although, the Pitta type is the most prone to develop gallstones, other body types are at risk, too if they regularly eat foods that go against their natural constitutional requirements (for further details about diets according to body-types see refer to a good book on Ayurveda or to *"The Key to Health and Rejuvenation"*). What upsets all the body types though, are processed, preserved, and unnatural foods and drinks. Foods which contain artificial sweeteners such as aspartame or saccharine, also upset liver functions. Drinking alcohol on a regular basis causes fat deposits in the liver, and so does eating foods that contain a lot of sugar. The increased consumption of sugar among children may explain why such a high percentage of children today have already accumulated numerous gallstones in the liver, although only few children normally develop stones in the gall bladder at this age (I have given the liver cleanse to many ill children, all of whom have released hundreds of gallstones). Children rarely produce gallstones when being on a balanced, vegetarian diet, rich in fruits, vegetables, and complex carbohydrates.

Dehydration

Many people today suffer dehydration without being aware of it. Dehydration is a condition when body cells no longer receive enough water, required for basic metabolic processes. The cells can run out of water for a number of reasons:

- Lack of water intake (anything less than one litre of water a day)
- Regular consumption of drinks that have a strong diuretic effect, e.g. coffee, tea, colas, soda, alcoholic beverages,
- Regular consumption of stimulating foods or substances such as meat, hot spices, chocolate, sugar, tobacco, narcotic drugs, etc.
- Stress
- Excessive exercise
- Overeating and excessive weight
- Most medical drugs
- Watching television for several hours

Any of these factors can deprive the body cells of water, which coerces them to hold on to water. They do this by increasing the thickness of their membranes. Although this emergency measure may "save" some water, it also reduces the cells' ability to absorb new water as well as nutrients. Some of the unabsorbed water (and nutrients) is accumulated in the connective tissues surrounding the cells, causing swelling of the body and water retention in the legs, kidneys, face, eyes, arms, and other parts. At the same time, the blood plasma and lymph fluid becomes thick. Dehydration affects the natural fluidity of bile and thereby promotes the formation of gallstones.

Tea, coffee, cola or chocolate share the same nerve toxin (stimulant) *caffeine. Caffeine,* which is readily released into the blood, triggers a powerful immune response that helps to counteract and eliminate this nerve toxin. The energising or invigorating effect that arises from taking any of these stimulants is caused by this sudden increase in immune activity. Those who take these stimulants on a regular basis "get used to them" i.e. are no longer efficient enough, because excessive secretions of *cortisol* and *adrenaline drastically suppress* the immune system. Hence people have to take more of them to still get some of the "benefits."

Since the body cells have to continuously sacrifice some of their water for the removal of the nerve toxin *caffeine*, regular consumption of coffee, tea or colas causes them to become dehydrated. Note that for every cup of tea or coffee you drink the body has to mobilise about 3 cups of water, just to remove the stimulants, a luxury it cannot afford. This also applies to soft drinks, drugs or any other stimulants, including watching TV for many hours (see section "Lifestyle").

Rapid Weight Loss

Overweight people are at greater risk of developing gallstones than people of average weight. It is an undisputed fact that there are significant health benefits to be gained from losing excess pounds. For example many people can reduce high blood pressure and cholesterol levels through weight loss.

However, rapid weight loss through diet programmes advising very low intake of calories each day increases a person's risk of developing gallstones both in the liver and gall bladder. Some low-calorie diets may not contain enough fat to cause the gall bladder to contract enough to empty its bile. A meal or snack containing approximately 10 grams (one-third of an ounce) of fat is necessary for the gall bladder to contract normally. If this doesn't happen, there is bile retention in the gall bladder, leading to stone formation.

Obesity is associated with increased cholesterol secretion in the bile, thus an increased risk of cholesterol gallstones. When obese individuals undergo rapid or substantial weight loss due to one-sided diet programmes, the congested and therefore malnourished body seeks to take nutrient and fat components from reserve depots, which quickly raises blood fats and further increases the risk of gallstone formation. The sudden stone formation appears to be a result of increased cholesterol and decreased bile salts in the bile of these patients during rapid weight loss programmes.

Also gallstones are common among obese patients who lose weight rapidly after gastric bypass surgery. (In gastric bypass surgery, the size of the stomach is reduced, preventing the person from overeating.) One study found that more than a third (38 percent) of patients who had gastric bypass surgery developed gallstones afterward. Gallstones are most likely to occur within the first few months after surgery. The research findings relate, however, only to gallstones in the liver. The damage done to the liver itself through this procedure is likely to be far greater than causing gallstones in the gall bladder.

If substantial or rapid weight loss increases the risk of developing gallstones, more gradual weight loss would seem to lessen the risk of getting gallstones. In fact, if weight loss is concentrated more on regulating the times of eating and removing toxic waste deposits from the body, including gallstones from the liver and gall bladder, weight loss is *not* increasing the risk of gall bladder disease but is *reducing* it. By eliminating all stones from the liver and gall bladder an obese person can drastically improve digestive functions and gain energy rather than waste. This will cut out all harmful side effects that may be associated with sudden weight-loss.

Low Fat Diets

The promotion of a low fat diet as *the most healthy diet of all* can be held partly responsible for the continuos increase in liver and gall bladder disease among the population in the Western hemisphere. Until recently high protein foods were heralded as the most important food to provide physical strength and vitality. Fats, on the other hand, have been branded a culprit for causing many of today's chronic diseases. But fats themselves can certainly not be held responsible for causing, for example, heart disease.

At the beginning of the 20th century, heart attacks rarely occurred anywhere in the world. Since then fat consumption per capita has remained almost the same. But what has risen most dramatically in the affluent parts of the world, particularly since World War II, is the consumption of proteins. Overconsumption of protein foods have caused an unprecedented number of circulatory diseases and fatalities through heart attacks which by contrast still rarely occur among ethnic groups that mostly live on vegetarian foods. In a report by the American Medical Association it was stated that a vegetarian diet could prevent 97% of all cases of thrombosis leading to heart attacks.

Although the vegetarian diet may contain large amounts of fats, the fats don't seem to have any detrimental effects on the circulatory system. By contrast, overeating proteins of animal origin causes thickening of liver blood vessels, which leads to gallstone formation (see also section "Heart" Disease, *Circulatory Disorders*); gallstones cut down bile production in the liver. Diminished bile secretions reduce the body's ability to digest fats. Due to indigestion, weight gain, and other discomforts arising therefrom, a person is then naturally advised to cut down on fats. But this further prevents the gall bladder from completely emptying its bile contents, which lead to more problems with fat digestion. Eventually, the body will run short of useful essential fats. This prompts the liver to increase cholesterol production and more stones are formed. The less fat the body receives with the food the worse the situation becomes. But since fats cannot be digested properly, the body enters a vicious circle, which in most cases can only be stopped by removing *all* gallstones from the liver and gall bladder, and then gradually increasing fat intake to normal levels.

Low fat milk, for example, may be one of the culprits that start off this vicious cycle. Milk has been designed in such a way that it contains the right amounts of fats required for the digestion of milk proteins. Without the natural quantity of fat in the milk, the gall bladder is not stimulated to release the right amount of bile required to digest both the milk proteins and the milk fats. Hence undigested proteins and fats are left in the gastrointestinal tract causing severe putrefaction and lymphatic congestion, as often seen among milk formula-fed babies suffering intestinal colic. This may be responsible for the formation of gallstones in the liver of very young children. Even the *whole fat milk* offered in food stores today has a reduced fat content, certainly not sufficient to make milk digestible for most people. (For further details about the dangers involved in eating low fat or "light" foods, see "The Key to Health and Rejuvenation."

Hormone Replacement Therapy (HRT) and Birth Control Pills

The risk of cholesterol gallstones is higher among women, especially in those who have been using birth control pills and hormone replacements. According to research, oral contraceptives and other *oestrogens* double a woman's chance of developing gallstones (Bo Gyn, 1994; 83:5-11). The female hormone *oestrogen* contained in contraceptive pills and hormone replacements increases bile cholesterol and decreases gall bladder contraction. This *oestrogen* effect may thus not only be responsible for causing gallstones in the liver and gall bladder but also for many other diseases that arise from diminished liver functions. Earlier research also implicated *progestogens* contained in HRT drugs in the development of gallstones (Res Comm in Chem Path & Pharm, 1992; 75 [1]:69-84).

Women who go through the menopause can find great relief from menopausal symptoms by doing a series of liver cleanses. A better liver performance and an increased production of bile in particular can prevent and reverse osteoporosis and other bone/joint problems if diet and life-style are balanced as well.

Other Drugs

Medications prescribed to lower body lipids, such as *clofibrate* (ATROMID-S) and other cholesterol-lowering drugs, may increase cholesterol in the bile and lead to an increased risk of gallstones. These drugs lower blood fats, which they are designed to accomplish. This, however, leads the liver cells to assume that the body is short in fats; hence they produce more cholesterol which is secreted into the bile. The imbalanced composition of bile (excessive cholesterol) causes gallstones, both in the liver and in the gall bladder. *Octretide,* one of the new generation "statin" drugs, prevents the gall bladder from emptying after a fatty meal leaving plenty of bile there to form into stones. The dangers involved in such methods of interference are obvious, certainly more serious than having risen blood fats (contrary to common belief, there is no scientific evidence to date that shows heart disease is caused by high blood fats).

Certain antibiotics like *ceftriaxone,* used for lower respiratory tract infections, skin and urinary tract infections, pelvic inflammatory disease, bone and joint infections as well as meningitis also cause gallstone formation, according to several studies published in various medical journals such as the Lancet, 1988 (ii: 1411-3) and 1989 (i: 165).

Similarly, anti-rejection drugs given to kidney and heart transplant patients increases the likelihood of forming gallstones. Also *thiazides,* which are water pills used for high blood pressure, may bring on gall bladder disease in patients with gallstones. Children taking *furosemide* are likely to develop gallstones, according to research published in the *Journal of Perinatology*, 1992, 12 [2}: 107-11). *Prostaglandins* have no fewer side effects.

All drugs are toxic by nature and require detoxification by the liver, yet impaired liver function permits many of the poisonous chemicals to enter the bile. This alters the natural balance of its constituents and leads to gall bladder formation in the liver and, in some instances also in the gall bladder. The above findings only refer to gallstones in the gall bladder and don't reveal the severity of damage that these drugs can cause to the liver itself. Before drugs can cause the development of several gallstones in the gall bladder, they must have caused hundreds of them in the liver bile ducts.

Symptomatic treatments always have a price tag attached to them, that is the impairment of basic liver functions. It is far more beneficial for the body to remove all the gallstones, restore normal blood values and improve digestion of food and elimination of waste than to suppress symptoms. Symptoms are *not* the disease, they only indicate that the body requires immediate care and attention.

3. Lifestyle

Disrupting the Biological Clock

The way we organise and live our lives has a great impact on how our body functions. Its efficiency and performance largely depends on set biological rhythms that are in synchrony with the so-called *circadian rhythms.* Circadian rhythms are closely associated with the movements of our planet around the sun and its axis as well as the motions of the moon and other planets in relation to the position of the earth.

Our body has more than 100 such 24-hour rhythms. Each individual rhythm controls the timing of an aspect of our body's functions, including heart rate, blood pressure, body temperature, hormone levels, secretion of digestive juices and even pain threshold. All these rhythms are well co-ordinated with other and are controlled by the brain's "pacemaker device" called *suprachiasmatic nuclei.* This area of the brain regulates the firing of nerve cells that seem to set our biological rhythms. If one rhythm becomes disrupted somehow, other rhythms are thrown off balance too. There are in fact numerous disorders that can arise when one or more of our biological rhythms are interfered with through mistakes in our lifestyle.

This section deals with some of the most common "deviations" that particularly affect the functioning of our liver and gall bladder. By attuning our daily routine to the natural schedule of our body we can greatly assist it in its ceaseless effort to nourish, cleanse and heal itself and also prevent new health problems from arising in the future.

The Natural Sleep/Wake Cycles

Our natural sleep/wake cycles are regulated by the alteration of day and night. The onset of daylight triggers, for example, the release of powerful hormones *(glucocorticoids)* of which the main ones are *cortisol* and *corticosterone*. Their secretion has marked circadian variations. The hormones regulate some of the most important functions in the body, including metabolism, blood sugar level and immune responses. Peak levels are between 4 and 8 a.m. and gradually decrease as the day continues. The lowest level occurs between midnight and 3 a.m.

If you change your daily sleep/wake schedule by sleeping, for example, after midnight versus 2 hours before midnight and waking after 8 or 9 a.m. versus rising with the sun at around 6 a.m., the peak of *cortisol's* cycle changes accordingly. This can create chaotic conditions in the body. Toxic waste materials that have accumulated in the rectum and the urinary bladder during the night, normally meant to be eliminated between 6 and 8 a.m., are partially retained and reabsorbed. When you disrupt your normal sleep/wake cycles, the body's rhythms influenced by sleep become desynchronised with those regulated by darkness/daylight. This can lead to almost every type of disorder, including chronic liver, respiratory and heart diseases.

An upset *cortisol* cycle can also bring on acute problems. It has been found that more strokes and heart attacks occur in the morning than at any other time of day. Blood clots form most rapidly at about 8 am. Blood pressure also rises in the morning and stays elevated until late afternoon. At around 6 p.m. it drops off and hits its lowest point during the night. To support the basic hormonal and circulatory rhythms in the body, it is therefore best to sleep early (before 10 p.m.) and rise not later than the sun does (ideally at around 6 a.m.).

One of the *pineal gland's* most powerful hormones is the neurotransmitter *melatonin*. The secretion of *melatonin* starts between 9.30 - 10.30 P.M. (depending on age), inducing sleepiness. It reaches peak levels between 2am-3am and drops to its lowest levels at midday. The pineal gland controls reproduction, sleep and motor activity, blood pressure, the immune system, the pituitary and thyroid glands, cellular growth, body temperature, and many other vital functions. All of them depend on the regular *melatonin* cycle, which can be disrupted by sleeping late or working night shifts.

The brain also synthesises *serotonin*, which is an important neurotransmitter relating to our state of well being. It affects day and night rhythms, sexual behaviour, memory, appetite, impulsiveness, fear, and even suicidal tendencies. Unlike *melatonin, serotonin* increases with the light of the day; physical exercise and sugar also stimulate it. If we get up late in the morning, lack of exposure to enough daylight reduces *serotonin* levels during the day and, since *melatonin* is a breakdown product of *serotonin*, also the levels of *melatonin* during the night.

Any deviation from the circadian rhythm causes abnormal secretions of the brain hormones *melatonin* and *serotonin*. This in turn leads to erratic biological rhythms, which can subsequently disrupt the harmonious functioning of the entire organism, including metabolism and hormonal balance. Suddenly, we may feel 'out of tune' and become susceptible to develop a range of disorders from a simple headache or depression to a fully-grown tumour.

Also production of growth hormones which stimulate growth in children and help maintain muscle and connective tissue in adults depends on proper sleep cycles. Sleep triggers hormone production with peaks occurring during the first two hours of sleep before midnight (coinciding with dreamless sleep, called "beauty sleep"). If you're sleep deprived, production drops. People who work the night shift have a greater incidence of insomnia, infertility, cardiovascular illness and stomach problems. Also performance falls and accident rates are higher during the night.

Meal Times

Ayurveda declared thousands of years ago that in order to maintain physical and emotional well being the body must be fed according to a natural time schedule. Like most other functions in the body, the digestive process is controlled by circadian rhythms, too. The secretions of bile and other digestive juices peak at midday and are at their lowest during the night. Hence it is best to eat the largest meal of the day at around midday and only light meals during breakfast and dinner. This enables the body to digest the ingested food properly and absorb the right amount of nutrients for the maintenance of proper functions throughout the body. To avoid interfering with the secretion of digestive juices at lunchtime, it is best to eat breakfast not later than 8 a.m. Dinner is digested most effectively when eaten between 6 and 7 p.m.

Any long-term disruption of this cycle, either caused by irregular eating habits, or by placing the main emphasis on dinner and/or breakfast leads to accumulation of undigested foods, lymph and blood congestion. This also disrupts our natural instinct which would naturally tempt us to eat only those foods that are suitable for our personal body type and to eat them when we can digest them best. The large amounts of undigested and unused foods eaten at the wrong times of the day impair the digestive functions further and cause gallstones in the liver and gall bladder (see digestive disorders).

4. Other Causes

Watching Television for Several Hours

Research has shown that watching television can dramatically increase cholesterol production in the body. This applies especially to children who may show a rise of up to 300% cholesterol within a few hours of watching television. Such excessive secretions of cholesterol alter the composition of bile, which causes formation of gallstones in the liver.

Exposure to television is a great challenge for the brain. It is far beyond its capacity to process the flood of incoming stimuli that emanate from the overwhelming number of picture frames appearing on the TV screen every split of a second. The resulting strain takes its toll. Blood pressure rises to help move more oxygen, glucose, cholesterol, vitamins, and other nutrients around the body and to the brain, all of which are used up rapidly by the heavy brainwork. Add violence, suspense and the noise of gunshots etc., to the spectacle and the adrenal glands respond with shots of adrenaline to prepare the body for a 'fight or flight'. This in turn contracts large and small blood vessels in the body, causing a shortage of water, sugar, and other nutrients in the cells.

The signs for such an effect can be many. You may feel shattered, exhausted, stiff in neck and shoulders, very thirsty, lethargic, depressed, and even too tired to go to sleep. Stress, for example, triggers cholesterol production in the body. Since cholesterol is the basic ingredient of stress hormones in the body, stressful situations use up large quantities of cholesterol which stimulates the liver to produce more of it to make up for the loss. If our body did not bother to increase cholesterol levels during such stress encounters, we would have millions of television deaths by now. Still, the stress response comes with a number of side effects, one of which is the formation of gallstones.

Emotional Stress

A stressful lifestyle can alter the flora of the bile and thereby cause formation of gallstones in the liver. One of the most stress-causing factors in life is not having enough time for oneself. Not having enough time creates pressure, continuous pressure causes frustration and frustration turns into anger. Anger is an indication of severe stress. Its effect on the body can be measured by the amounts of adrenaline and noradrenaline secreted into the blood by the adrenal glands. These hormones help the body to deal with excitement and stressful situations.

Under stress, the hormones increase the rate and force of the heart beat, raise blood pressure and constrict the blood vessels in the secretory glands of the digestive system. In addition, they restrict the flow of digestive juices, including stomach acids and bile, delay onward movement and absorption of food, and inhibit the elimination of urine and faeces. When food is no longer digested properly and significant amounts of waste are prevented from leaving the body via the excretory organs, almost every area of the body begins to be affected, including the liver and gall bladder. Chronic stress, or rather the inability to cope with it, can be held responsible for 85-95 of all diseases, commonly referred to as *psychosomatic* diseases.

During relaxation, on the other hand, all these (disrupted) functions can be normalised again, unless the stress-caused obstructions require deep cleansing. The best antidote to dealing with stress and its harmful effects are methods of relaxation, such as meditation, yoga, or spending time in nature. To cope with the fast pace of modern life and give the nervous system enough time to relax all these restricted functions or keep them balanced it is vital to spend at least 1 hour a day in silence. If you had any stressful periods in your life or have a difficult time calming down or unwinding, you will greatly benefit doing the liver cleanse first. Having gallstones in the liver is by itself a major cause for constant stress responses in the body. By eliminating them, you will become naturally calm and relaxed. You will also discover that you become much less angry or upset than before once your liver is clean, regardless of the situation or circumstances.

Conventional Treatments for Gallstones

Conventional treatments for gallstones aim at either dissolving gallstones in the gall bladder or removing the gall bladder through surgery. These treatments have, however, no effect on the large numbers of stones congesting the bile ducts of the liver. The uncontrolled flow of bile into the gall bladder, resulting from gall bladder surgery, for example, leads to further problems with digesting and absorbing food, particularly if it contains fats. The result is that an ever-increasing amount of toxic waste is accumulated in the intestinal tract and lymphatic system. The inability to properly digest fat and assimilate fat stimulates the liver cells to increase their production of cholesterol, the side effect of which is seen in a drastic increase of cholesterol stones in the liver, causing further complications throughout the body.

Any treatment of the gall bladder, however advanced and sophisticated it may be, can only be considered *a drop in the ocean* because it does not remove the main problem, that is the blockage of bile ducts by hundreds or thousands of gallstones in the liver.

Dissolving Gallstones

For patients with mild, infrequent symptoms or those who do not want surgery a number of different drugs are available which claim to dissolve gallstones. On the surface it seems like a good idea to gradually dissolve gallstones through drugs that contain bile salts (oral dissolution therapy). Given in pill form over twelve months, the drugs may decrease the amount of cholesterol in the bile. But according to the British Medical Journal (BMJ, 1995; 311:99-105) the use of bile salts has a failure rate as high as 50 per cent. In addition, many of the "successful" patients simply do not experience complete gallstone dissolution. For the few patients who do, the recurrence rate can be as high as 50 per cent. Other dissolving agents such as *methyl tert-butyl* ether have no advantages over bile salts. Unsuccessful treatment may lead to surgery.

More recently, solvents have been directly instilled into the gall bladder by means of a small catheter placed through the skin. This has been shown to be very effective in dissolving cholesterol stones but does not resolve the major issue -- the accumulation of gallstones in the liver. There is not enough scientific research yet to determine the side effects that may accompany this method of treatment.

Shock Waves

Another alternative method to surgery is "lithotripsy", a technique where the gallstones are literally pounded into submission by a series of sound waves. In a 1993 report by the *Lancet,* this therapy has great set backs because it can result in kidney damage and raise blood pressure. Both these effects can lead to an increase in the number of gallstones in the liver (see Disorders of the Circulatory and Urinary Systems, Chapter 2). In addition, this procedure during which gallstones are fragmented through shock waves, leaves toxic gallstone residue behind which becomes a home for bacteria, causing infection possibly anywhere in the body. Recent studies have confirmed that most patients undergoing this treatment experience internal bleeding, ranging from a small haemorrhage to major bleeding that requires blood transfusion. The treatment also has a high stone recurrence rate.

Surgery

In 1991, 600,000 Americans had their gall bladder removed through surgical intervention. While open gall bladder surgery (cholecystectomy) is still commonly used for patients with frequent or severe pain, or with a history of acute *cholecystitis,* laparoscopic cholecystectomy has now become the preferred surgical technique. With traditional surgery, the gall bladder is removed through an open technique requiring a standard skin incision and general anaesthesia. During laparoscopic cholecystectomy or "keyhole operation", the stone-filled gall bladder is literally pulled through a small incision in the abdomen. Sometimes open cholecystectomy is required if a keyhole operation fails.

With keyhole operation, patients seem to recover much faster and often leave the hospital and return to regular activity within days. However, since its introduction, this *"band aid"* approach to treating gall bladder disease has prompted many patients to have a gall bladder operation unnecessarily, that is to get rid of some persistent symptoms of discomfort. Apart from having had no effect on the overall mortality rate from gall bladder diseases, laparoscopic surgery does have its risks. Complications arising from the procedure include haemorrhage, inflammation of the pancreas, a potentially fatal condition, and perforation of the duodenal wall (New England Journal of Medicine, 1996; 335: 961). There may be injury and obstruction of bile ducts and leakage of bile into the abdomen, causing serious infection. About one in a hundred patients are at risk of dying from this kind of operation.

Bile-duct injuries have increased dramatically as a result of using keyhole surgery. In Ontario, Canada, where 86% of gall bladder operations are performed in this way, the number of bile-duct injuries has risen by 305 per cent (Lancet, February, 1996).

In a number of patients gallstones are caught in the common bile duct (the main bile duct leading to the duodenum). In such cases, the removal of the gall bladder will not alleviate the symptoms of gallstone disease. To help the condition, a flexible tube is placed in the mouth and is advanced to the point where the common bile enters the duodenum. During the procedure, the opening of the bile duct is enlarged and the stones are moved into the small intestines. Unfortunately, many of the stones may become stuck in the small or large intestines, becoming a source of constant intestinal infection or related problems.

Since any of these procedures do not address the cause of gall bladder disease at all, they in actual fact contribute to further disruption of the digestive and eliminative processes in the body. The short-term relief that a patient can experience after his gall bladder has been removed, may cause the patient to believe that he has been cured, whereas in truth the continuous impairment of proper bile secretion may lead to the development of more serious health problems than gall bladder disease. The liver cleanse, on the other hand, painlessly removes not only the few gallstones in the gall bladder or the large bile ducts but also and most importantly those hundreds or thousands in the liver. It is extremely unfortunate, that millions of people had their gall bladder removed unnecessarily or have lost their lives because of liver and gallstone disease when a simple natural procedure like the liver cleanse could have restored their liver and gall bladder functions so easily and naturally.

Chapter 5

What can I expect from the Liver Cleanse?

A Disease-free Life

Disease is not part of our body's natural design. We become sick when our immune system is suppressed or overpowered by the accumulation of large amounts of toxic waste. This form of internal "suffocation" is almost always preceded or accompanied by a blockage of the liver bile ducts. When the liver, which is the major factory of the body, becomes congested with gallstones, disease is imminent.

By clearing the liver bile ducts from all obstructions and maintaining a balanced diet and lifestyle, the body can return to a state of balance, called health. The old saying "prevention is better than cure" applies very well to the liver. If the liver is kept free of gallstones, it is very difficult to upset this state of balance. Having a clean liver basically means a clean bill of health.

Both health insurance companies and their clients could greatly benefit from the liver cleanse in a number of ways. The companies would be able to lower their premium rates and expenditure considerably while the insured population would enjoy much better health, have fewer losses of working days due to illness, and avoid the fear and pain that accompanies disease. The older generation would no longer be considered such a burden, as they would be able to take care of themselves more and more rather than less and less. Health care costs could be cut down drastically which may be the only way to safeguard continued progress and prosperity in a nation like the United States. If the current trends of escalating health expenditures in the U.S. continue, the nation is likely to end up in bankruptcy. In 1992 health care costs in the U.S. exceeded the $800 billion mark. The projected health cost for the year 2000 is $1615,9 billion.

Health care is not about how much money is being made available for treating symptoms of disease. Treating the symptoms of an illness will always require further treatments in the future because the origins of disease remain obscure and become worse if unattended. The quick fix approach of suppressing symptoms of disease is the main cause of the spiralling health costs. Actually curing diseases and preventing new diseases from arising is comparatively very inexpensive. Conventional health care, as it exists today, is already unaffordable for many people and will become a rarely acquired privilege for most people in the near future. If the liver cleanse would be applied as a cure for gall bladder diseases in the United States alone, it could help the 20 million gallstone sufferers to live a normal, comfortable life and prevent related illnesses from arising in the future.

The liver cleanse, however, does much more than just restore gall bladder function, it helps a person to take active care of his health, for the rest of his life. Taking up an insurance against disease cannot guarantee a disease-free life. Perfect health develops naturally when you keep the body free of gallstones and other toxic waste deposits and when you fulfil the most basic requirements for maintaining youthfulness and vitality throughout life.

Improved Digestion, Energy and Vitality

The meaning of "good digestion" comprises three basic processes in the body:

1. The food we eat is broken down into its nutrient components.

2. The nutrients are readily absorbed, distributed to all the cells and metabolised efficiently.

3. The waste products resulting from the breakdown and utilisation of food are completely eliminated through the excretory organs.

The body requires a good digestion in order to guarantee the smooth and efficient turnover of its 60-100 trillion cells. Each day the body has to produce 30,000,000,000 new cells and replace them with the same number of old, worn or damaged cells. If this goes smoothly, day after day and year after year, the new generation of cells in the body will be as effective and healthy as the previous ones. Although, certain cells such as those of the brain and heart do not get replaced, their raw ingredients, i.e. the carbon, oxygen, hydrogen, and nitrogen atoms, are renewed within less than a year.

The natural turnover of cells or atoms, however, is no longer complete or efficient with the majority of people who live a in fast-paced world that has little time for a healthy lifestyle and for eating a balanced diet consisting of natural, unpolluted foods and fresh, clean water. Only a small number of societies living in very remote and secluded areas such as the Abkhasian Mountains in Southern Russia, the Himalayan Mountains, the Andes or Northern Mexico have managed to maintain their youth and health at any age level, even when over 100 years.

By cleansing the body and giving it the best possible treatment we can raise our quality of life to a high level of energy and vitality, which is the natural state of health that every human being deserves to have. A well functioning digestive system and gallstone-free liver provides the main condition through which the body can regulate the smooth turnover of cells without accumulating toxins.

Relieve of Pain

Pain is a signal the body uses to identify and correct a certain problem of malfunctioning. Pain is not a disease in itself but a sign of proper immune action. When the pain subsides naturally, without the use of painkillers, this shows that the body has returned to a state of balance. Chronic pain indicates that the immune response is not sufficient and the cause of the problem has not yet been removed.

Cleansing the liver and gall bladder from all gallstones can help reduce and eliminate pain in the body, regardless of whether it is felt in the joints, head, nerves, muscles, or organs. The body is as healthy as the blood is. If the blood contains large amounts of toxins, which is the case with a congested liver, there may be irritation, inflammation, and infection or further damage of cells and tissues in the weaker parts of body. If the functions of digestion, metabolism and elimination of waste material in the body are impaired due to weak liver performance then the blood immune system cannot accomplish complete healing, which becomes a source of further complications.

The healing response relies on an efficient immune system, most part of which is located in the intestinal tract. The liver which is the main organ controlling digestion and metabolism of food must be free of all obstructions (gallstones) to prevent the immune system from being overtaxed. If immunity is low in the intestines it will also be low in all the other parts of the body. Pain relief is automatic when congestion subsides and immunity returns to its full level of efficiency. Pain is not something that requires treatment, unless it is unbearable. If the cause of chronic pain is chronic congestion then the liver, intestines and any other excretory organ should be cleansed which in most cases will relieve pain and restore immunity.

A more Flexible Body

Physical flexibility is a measure as to how well the organs, joints, muscles, connective tissues and cells are nourished by the food we eat, the water we drink and the air we breathe. The digestive and metabolic processes that make these things available to the cells of the body need to be in top condition for health to be a permanent reality. Stiffness in joints and muscles indicate retention of acidic metabolic waste products due to impaired digestion and elimination.

Anyone who practices yoga, gymnastics or any other form of

exercise and does one or several liver cleanses notices a greatly increased flexibility of the spine, the joints and muscles. Deposits of mineral salts in the neck and shoulder areas begin to lessen and aches and stiffness disappear. The whole body feels more "connected" as the connective tissues that keep the cells together become more fluid again.

A river of pure water flows more easily and with less friction than a river that is thickened by a lot of filth and mud. One of the liver's most important functions is to keep the blood thin so that it can distribute nutrients to the cells, pick up waste materials, and carry messenger hormones to their destinations. Thick blood is the cause of most illnesses in the body and it can be recognised, among other symptoms, in the lack of flexibility of certain parts of the body. If the spine and joints are not flexible or are stiff and painful, this indicates that most internal organs suffer circulatory problems. Blood circulation greatly improves when gallstones seize to congest the liver. This leads to increased flexibility and mobility of the body. A good and regular exercise programme helps to support and maintain the newly found flexibility.

A flexible body indicates a flexible mind and a rigid body reflects a rigid mind. As the body is supplied with thinner blood and hardened structures begin to soften again, the mind also begins to become more free and flexible. This enhances our ability to flow with the opportunities of the present moment, adding tremendous joy and fulfilment to our life.

Reversal of the Ageing Process

Ageing is generally viewed as an unavoidable phenomenon that will afflict every person sooner or later. However, this viewpoint applies only to its negative effects. Ageing can also be seen as a growth process that makes life richer, increases wisdom and enhances experience and maturity, assets that are rarely found in young age. The negative aspect of the ageing process, however, which the majority of people identify with, is more a metabolic disorder that develops gradually over a period of time.

The unwanted effects of ageing result from a process of malfunction that occurs on the cellular level. When groups of cells are unable to remove their daily amounting metabolic waste material fast enough, some of it is deposited in the cell membranes. In due time this form of waste disposal becomes more pronounced and apparent. Retaining waste, which gradually cuts down the supply of oxygen, nutrients, and water to the cells, increasingly thickens the cell membranes. The cell membranes of a newborn baby are very thin, nearly colourless and transparent. The average 70-year-old person has cell membranes that are at least five times as thick as those are in a baby's body; the membranes' colour is brown and in some cases even black.

Although most cells in the body are replaced on a regular basis by new cells, the new cells are in not better off than the old ones. The tissues or groups of cells have become weaker and suffer malnutrition, giving the new generation of cells a poor start in life. Within a short period of time the cells' membranes become clogged up, too. They'll never get a chance to develop into healthy young cells. As more and more of the cells and the surrounding connective tissues become saturated with toxic substances, the organs in the body begin to age and deteriorate faster. The cell membranes become cellular "garbage bins". The skin, which is the largest organ in the body, also begins to suffer malnutrition. Consequently it looses some of its elasticity, changes its natural colour, becomes dry and rough, or develops blemishes that consist of metabolic waste products. At this stage, the negative aspect of the ageing process becomes visible on the outside. Yet external ageing, which is a direct result of defective cell metabolism, always occurs inside the body first.

Impaired digestion and liver function are the main causes of an inefficient cell metabolism. Both improve dramatically when all the gallstones in the liver and gall bladder are eliminated and other toxic waste materials are removed from the organs, tissues and cells through simple methods of cleansing (see chapter 7). When the cells begin to "shed" their "dark skins", the absorption of oxygen, nutrients, and water increases and with it their vitality and efficiency. As digestion and metabolism of food continues to improve, instead of being "old and tired," the cells will become "young and dynamic". This is the time when the actual ageing process is reversed and the positive aspects of ageing begin to dominate.

Inner and Outer Beauty

The results of a steadily improving cell metabolism will affect the way you feel about your inner self as much as it will show on the outside. Old people look young and radiant when they are truly healthy. Young people can look very old if their bodies are toxic and tired. So to develop outer beauty we must develop inner beauty first.

A body that has accumulated a lot of toxic waste material is not capable of giving us an inner sense of beauty and worthiness. There are still groups of indigenous people living in the more remote parts of the world who enjoy perfect health and vitality. They regularly purge their liver, kidneys, and intestines with oils, herbs and liquids. These practises have become lost to modern societies where the main emphasis is on improving the superficial physical appearance, and in the case of an illness, on fixing its symptom rather than removing the cause.

Those who have done a series of liver cleanses report that they feel much better about their body, their life and their environment. In many cases, a person's self-esteem and ability to appreciate others improves with an increased degree of purity in the body. The liver cleanse can greatly contribute towards increasing one's vitality and "inner beauty". This will not only slow or reverse the ageing process but also make you feel more youthful and attractive, whatever age you are.

Improved Emotional Health

The liver cleanse has direct implications on how you feel

about yourself and others. Under stress, you are likely to become irritable, annoyed and even angry and frustrated. Most people assume that stress has something to do with the problems they face in their lives. Yet this is only partially true. Our response to certain issues, situations, or people is only negative because we cannot cope with them.

The liver, which maintains the functions of the nervous system by supplying vital nutrients, also determines our stress response. Gallstones impede the proper distribution of nutrients, which forces the body to take recourse to several emergency measures including excessive secretion of stress hormones. For a short while, this helps to maintain most functions, but sooner or later the body's equilibrium becomes disturbed and the nervous system aggravated. Any external pressure or demanding situation may trigger an exaggerated stress response which may give rise to the feeling of being stressed or overwhelmed.

Our emotional health is intimately linked to our physical health. Cleansing the liver and keeping it clean helps maintain emotional balance. By removing the gallstones you also root out any deep seated anger and resentment that may have been stored there for a long time. This relief or letting go of past unresolved issues may create a new sense of being alive or euphoria almost immediately after a cleanse.

A Clearer Mind and Improved Creativity

Clarity of mind, memory recall, the ability to concentrate and focus attention, and creativity all depend on how well nourished and circulated the brain is. An ineffective circulatory system has a dulling effect on all the mental processes. This in turn can increase stress and strain on the nervous system.

With each new liver cleanse you will notice a further improvement of the mind. Many people report that their mind becomes less turbulent or more settled. Others report a sudden influx of creative thoughts that help to improve their work performance and creative output. Artists generally find that there is an opening of a new dimension to their creative expression and perception of colours, shapes and forms.

Those involved in techniques of spiritual growth or self-development will find that the elimination of all gallstones in the liver may help them access deeper and formerly hidden areas of themselves and utilise more of their mental potential. The liver cleanse helps balance the *solar plexus chakra*, which is the energy centre in the body responsible for will power, energy absorption and distribution, as well as liver, gall bladder, stomach, pancreas, and spleen functions. This central part of the body becomes a lot more comfortable after doing a liver cleanse.

Chapter 6

Simple Rules to Avoid Gallstones

1. Cleanse your Liver Twice a Year

After you have eliminated all your gallstones through a series of liver cleanses it is best to cleanse the liver twice a year. The best date for a liver cleanse is about one week before a seasonal change. Begin the liver cleanse at around the 15th of March, the 15th of June, the 15th of September or the 15th of December, with the actual day of the cleanse coinciding with an equinox of solstice day. Repeat six months later.

During the 10 days before and after a seasonal change the immune system is generally low which makes many people more susceptible towards catching a cold. This also is the time when gallstones in the liver and gall bladder tend to increase in number and size.

2. Avoid Overeating

The greatest cause of gallstones *is overindulging in foods and drinks*. One of the major methods of preventing gallstones therefore is "under-eating." Eating in moderation and an occasional "liquid day" (ideally once a week) help the digestive system to remain efficient and deal with any deposits of undigested foods. Liquids include vegetable soups, fruit juices, vegetable juices, herb teas and water. Leaving the dining table still a little hungry maintains a healthy desire for good nutritious foods, whereas overeating leads to congestion and cravings for *quick energy* foods or drinks such as sugar, sweets, chocolate, coffee, tea, and colas. All these foods or drinks lead to gallstone formation.

3. Reduce Your Intake of Alcohol

Alcohol is liquefied sugar. If a generally healthy person consumes, for example, 2 glasses of wine within an hour, the liver is not able to detoxify all the alcohol. Much of the alcohol is converted into fatty deposits and eventually gallstones in the liver. If the liver has already accumulated a certain number of gallstones, once alcohol is consumed they will grow faster and more plentiful in a shorter period of time.

Like coffee or tea, alcohol also has a strong dehydrating effect, which reduces the water content of the body's cells, blood, lymph , and bile, impairing blood circulation and elimination of waste products. The effects of a dehydrated central nervous system are delirium, blurred vision, loss of memory and orientation, slow reaction time, and what is generally described as "hangover." Under the influence of alcohol and subsequent dehydration, the nervous system becomes depressed which leads to a slowing of the digestive, metabolic and hormonal processes in the body. All this heads towards producing more and more gallstones in the liver and gall bladder.

Those who have had a history of gallstones better avoid alcohol altogether. Many of my patients who stopped drinking alcohol altogether, have spontaneously recovered from such problems as panic attacks, arrhythmia, respiratory problems, various heart conditions, gall bladder attacks, pancreas infection, prostate enlargement, colitis, and other inflammatory diseases. If you suffer any disease at all, it is best to stay away from any dehydrating beverages such as alcohol, coffee, tea, or sodas. This gives the body the maximum strength and efficiency that it requires to deal with and heal the affected part or parts of the body.

4. Drink Plenty of Water

To produce the 1,1 - 1,5 litres of bile a day, which the body requires for the digestion of food, the liver needs plenty of water. In addition, much water is used for maintaining proper blood volume, hydrating the cells and connective tissues, flushing out toxins, and many other functions. Since the body cannot store water as it can store fat, it is dependent on sufficient water intake.

To maintain proper bile production and bile consistency as well as balanced blood values you need to drink a minimum of 6-8 glasses of water a day. The ideal time to drink water is 1-2 glasses of (warm) water first thing in the morning, 1 glass of water (room temperature or warm) half an hour before each meal and 1 glass of water between 2 and 2 ½ hours after each meal. This ensures that blood, bile, and lymph remain fluid enough to conduct their respective activities in the body.

If you suffer from high blood pressure and use hypertensive drugs, make sure have your blood pressure monitored regularly as with the increase of water consumption it may return to normal within a short period of time. You may also loose weight if you are overweight and gain weight if you are underweight.

5. Have Regular Meal Times

The body is controlled by numerous circadian rhythms, which regulate the most important functions in the body according to pre-programmed time intervals. Sleep, secretion of hormones and digestive juices, elimination of waste, etc., all follow a specific routine. If the routine is disrupted more often than it is kept, the body becomes unbalanced and cannot fulfil its tasks according to the schedule dictated by the circadian rhythms.

Eating regular meals makes it easy for the body to prepare for the production and secretion of the right amounts of digestive juices for each meal. Irregular eating habits, on the other hand, confuse the body. It will be weakened by having to adjust itself to a new mealtime each time you eat a meal. Skipping meals here and there, eating at different times, or eating between mealtimes in particular disrupt the cycles of bile production by liver cells, leading to the development of gallstones.

By maintaining a regular routine of eating, the body's 60 trillion cells will be able to receive their daily ratio of nutrients according to schedule which helps cell metabolism to be smooth and effective. Many metabolic disorders such as diabetes or obesity result from irregular eating habits and can be improved by matching the eating times with the natural circadian rhythms. It is best to take the largest meal of the day at around midday and only light meals at breakfast (not later than 8 a.m.) and dinner (ideally not later than 7 p.m.).

6. Eat a Vegetarian Diet

Eating a balanced vegetarian diet is one of the most effective ways to prevent the formation of gallstones and prevent heart disease as well as cancer. If you feel you cannot solely live on foods that are of vegetable origin, then at least try to substitute red meat with chicken, rabbit or turkey. All forms of animal protein decrease the solubility of bile, which is a major risk factor for gallstones. By adding more vegetables, fruits and dietary fibre to your diet, you will reduce this risk. Aged cheese, commercial yoghurt (versus homemade yoghurt) as well as processed and refined foods cause unbalanced bile. Certainly avoid fried and deep fried foods. Also the heated oils used in fast food restaurant are a quick way to produce gallstones.

7. Drink Ionised Water Frequently

Drinking ionised water has a deep cleansing effect on the tissues of the body; it helps reduce overall toxicity, improves circulatory functions and balances bile. Water becomes charged with negative oxygen ions by boiling it for a certain length of time. Boil water for 15-20 minutes and pour it in a thermos flask which keeps it hot and ionised. Take 1-2 sips every half hour throughout the day and drink it as hot as you drink tea.

The oxygen ions are generated through the bubbling effect of boiling water, similar to water falling on the ground or breaking against the shore. In the thermos flask, the water will stay ionised for up to 12 hours or as long it is hot.

When ionised water is ingested through frequent sips throughout the day, it begins to systematically cleanse the tissues of the body and help rid it of positively charged hydrogen ions (those associated with high acidity and toxins). If you have excessive body weight, this cleansing method alone can help you shed many pounds of body-waste in a short time without the side effects that normally accompany sudden weight loss.

8. Avoid "Light-food" Products

There are many studies which show that *light-foods* encourage appetite and overeating and do **not** reduce weight; on the contrary, they may lead to weight gain. The more *enzymatic energy* is contained in food, the faster we feel satisfied and the more efficiently the food is turned into energy and nutrients.

By contrast, low calorie *light-foods* impair bile secretion, digestion and excretory functions. High levels of blood fats indicate that bile secretions are low, blood vessel walls have become thick and fats are no longer adequately digested and absorbed. Hence such a person suffers "fat deficiency." A low-fat diet may further increase cholesterol production in the liver, which is necessary to meet the greater demand for fats in the cells and tissues of the body. The side effects of this emergency response are development of gallstones, weight gain or wasting.

Low fat, low calorie diets are damaging to health and should if at all only be given in acute liver and gall bladder disorders when digestion and absorption of fats severely disrupted. After removing all gallstones and normalising liver functions, it is necessary to increase fat and calorie consumption again to meet the high-energy demands of the human physiology. Keeping consumption of fats and other high energy low for a longer period of time affects basic metabolic and hormonal processes in the body, which may have serious repercussions for one's health. A low protein diet helps to clear up the blood vessels, which will make normal fat intake no longer a risk for developing gall bladder or liver problems.

9. Getting Enough Sleep

Tiredness precedes any type of disease, whether it is cancer, heart disease or AIDS. Although impaired liver functions or low immunity may also cause fatigue, in most cases it is due to lack of sleep. Most tiredness results from lack of *before-midnight sleep* (and overeating).

The most powerful processes of purification and rejuvenation in the body are initiated during the two hours of sleep before midnight. Physiologically, there are two very different types of sleep, as verified by brain wave measurements, i.e., the *before-midnight sleep* and the *after-midnight sleep*. The first one includes deep sleep, often referred to as "Beauty Sleep," lasting for over one hour from about 11pm to midnight. During this time you are in a dreamless state of sleep where oxygen consumption in the body drops by about 8 percent. The rest that you gain during this hour of dreamless sleep is nearly three times deeper than what you get during the sleep after midnight when oxygen consumption in the body rises again.

Deep sleep never occurs after midnight and it comes only if you go to sleep at least two hours before midnight. If you miss out on deep sleep regularly, your body and mind become overtired and the stress responses are high. The stress responses include the secretions of the stress hormones *adrenaline, cortisol*, or *cholesterol* (a part of the cholesterol secreted during a stress response may end up in the form of gallstones). To keep these artificially derived energy bursts going, you may feel the urge to use such stimulants as cigarettes, coffee, tea, candy, cokes, alcohol, etc. When the body's energy reserves are finally exhausted chronic fatigue results.

When you feel tired, not only your mind is tired; all your body cells, your organs, your digestive system, etc., will suffer from lack of energy and are not able to function properly. When you are tired, your brain no longer receives adequate amounts of water, glucose, oxygen and amino acids, which serve as its main food. This situation can lead to innumerable problems in mind, body, and behaviour.

Doctors at the University of California, San Diego, have found that losing a few hours of sleep not only makes you feel tired during the next day but can also affect the immune system, possibly impairing the body's ability to fight infection. Since immunity diminishes with tiredness, your body is unable to defend itself against bacteria, microbes, and viruses and cannot cope with the build-up of toxic substances in the body.

Getting enough sleep, therefore, is the most important prerequisite for restoring health of body and mind. Try to sleep before 10 p.m. and get up between 6 and 7 a.m., or earlier, depending on your sleep requirements. Removing all the gallstones from the liver and gall bladder and getting enough sleep will reduce any tiredness that may be there during the day. Should the problem continue to prevail, the kidneys may need to be cleansed as well (to dissolve kidney stones see the book *"The Key to Health and Rejuvenation"*).

10. Avoid Overworking

Working too hard and too many hours overtaxes the body's energy system. Overworking stresses particularly the liver, which tries to convert as much complex sugar into simple sugars (glucose) to meet the excessive demand for energy in the brain or other parts of the body. If there is a shortfall of energy or energy supplies run out altogether, the body has to take recourse to such emergency measures as the stress response, which makes extra energy available but at the same time disrupts circulatory and immune functions.

The continuous secretion of adrenaline and other stress hormones that occurs in a person who "never stops working" can eventually make him become a *workaholic*. This is a condition when work has become the major source of excitement in a person's life. The excitement is provided be the "thrill" effect of the stress hormones.

To avoid exhausting your liver and damaging your immune system, make enough time for yourself. Try to allocate at least one hour a day for mediation, yoga, exercise or being in nature. The body is not a machine that can run continuously without having a break. Overworking the body and the mind in any way will eventually demand extra time for recovery from an illness. In the long run, overworking as a means to get things achieved faster or earn more money more quickly, cuts years off one's life and life off one's years.

The liver is designed to provide energy for a certain number of years; overextending this "service" of the liver damages or destroys it prematurely. By living moderately with regard to eating, sleeping, and working, the body can maintain an efficient energy system throughout life. An old saying recommends that we spend one third of our life sleeping, one third working, and one third for recreational activities. This formula maintains balance on all levels of life, mind, body, and spirit. Overworking upsets it.

11. Take Regular Exercise

Our technological and economic advancement has led to an increasingly sedentary lifestyle, which requires additional forms of physical movement to keep our bodies vital and healthy. Regular exercise helps us to increase our capacity to digest food, eliminate physical and emotional impurities, promote firmness and suppleness and strengthen our ability to deal with stressful situations. When performed in moderation, exercise is a great immune stimulant and improves neuromuscular integration in all age groups. Its effect of boosting self-confidence and self-esteem stems from the improved oxygen supply to the cells and the resulting well being in all parts of the body and mind.

The liver especially seems to benefit from aerobic forms of exercising. The increased availability of oxygen during and after exercising greatly improves circulation and particularly enhances the flow of venous blood from the liver towards the heart. A sedentary life style slows this process and causes stagnation of blood flow in the liver, leading to the development of gallstones. Thus regular, non-strenuous exercise can prevent new stones from forming.

On the other hand, any form of physical exertion resulting from over-exercising results in the secretion of abnormal amounts of stress hormones such as *adrenaline,* which may leave the body restless and shaky. When the body is depleted of energy, it is unable to do the repair work that arises from the strenuous workout, leaving the cardiovascular system weak and vulnerable to other stress factors. The thymus gland, which activates *lymphocytes* (immune cells that defend us against disease) and controls energy supplies, may shrink in size and cause the body to be agitated and vulnerable to all sorts of health problems.

Chose a form of exercise that gives you a sense of joy and satisfaction. Whenever you exercise make certain that you always breathe through your nose and keep your mouth closed, this will avoid the harmful *"adrenaline breathing."* Aerobic exercises are good as long as one maintains nose breathing (versus mouth breathing). If you run out of breath, slow down or stop exercising. You may resume the exercise once your breath is back to normal. This simple advice will prevent you from any harm that may arise from exercising.

Try to exercise every day, even if it is only for 10 minutes. It is important, though, not to do more than 50% of your capacity for exercise, the main thing is not to become tired. For example if you can swim for 30 minutes before you get tired, swim only for 15 minutes, etc. In time, your capacity for more exercise will unfold. Remember, both excessive exercising and lack of exercise weaken the immune system, impair liver functions and flood the blood with toxic chemicals.

12. Sunlight Lowers Cholesterol and Prevents Disease

Our body is capable of synthesising vitamin D by the action of the ultraviolet rays of the sun on a form of cholesterol in the skin. Regular exposure to sunlight has been shown to reduce cholesterol when required. But unlike cholesterol-lowering drugs, sunlight does *not* increase cholesterol in the bile, which is a major cause of gallstones. Sunlight rather has a holistic effect, meaning that all functions in the body can benefit. Ultraviolet light has proved to lower blood pressure, improve cardiac output, increase glycogen (complex sugar) stores in liver, balance blood sugar, improve the body's resistance to infections (increase of lymphocytes and phagocytic index), enhance oxygen carrying capacity of the blood and increase sex hormones among many other health promoting effects.

Sunbathing may be harmful, however, for those who live on a diet rich in acid-forming, highly processed foods and refined fats or their products. Also alcohol, cigarettes, and other mineral and vitamin-depleting substances such as allopathic and hallucinogenic drugs can make the skin vulnerable to ultraviolet radiation. After having cleared the liver and gall bladder from all gallstones moderate sun exposure will cause no harm. During the summer period it is best to avoid the sun between 10.00 a.m. and 3.00 p.m., whereas in winter and spring the same period may be beneficial for the body.

For maximum benefits it is best to take a shower before sunbathing. Don't use sunscreens as they cancel out the sun's positive effects. Start your sunlight treatment by exposing your entire body (if possible) for a few minutes to begin with and then increase the time each day by a few more minutes until you reach 20-30 minutes during each exposure. Alternatively, walking in the sun for an hour has similar benefits. This will give you enough sunlight to keep your body and mind healthy, provided you incorporate the basic aspects of a balanced diet and lifestyle.

13. Keep your Colon Clean

A weak, irritated and congested large intestine is a breeding place for bacteria, which break down waste and produce large amounts of noxious substances. Some of the toxins produced by the bacteria enter the blood, which takes them straight to the liver. Constant exposure of liver cells to these toxins impairs their performance and reduces bile secretion, which leads to further disruption of digestive functions.

Keeping the colon clean through *colonic irrigation*, for example, is an effective preventive method to safeguard the liver against toxins generated in the large intestine. *Colonic irrigation*, also known as *Colon Hydrotherapy*, is perhaps one of the most effective colon therapies since as within a 30-50 minute session it can eliminate large amounts of trapped waste that took many years to accumulate. During a *colonic irrigation* a total of 2-6 litres of distilled water is used to gently flush the colon. Through gentle abdominal massage, old deposits of mucoid faecal matter are loosened and subsequently removed with the water.

Colonics have a "relieving" effect. There will be a feeling of lightness, cleanness, and increased clarity of mind following a colonic, although during the procedure you may feel a slight discomfort from time to time whenever larger quantities of toxic waste detach themselves from the intestinal walls and move towards the rectum.

Colonic irrigation is a completely safe and hygienic system of cleansing the colon. Rubber tubing carries water into the colon and waste out of the colon. The released waste material can be seen floating through a tube, showing the type and quantity of waste eliminated.

Once the colon has been thoroughly cleansed through 2-3 or more colonics, then diet, exercise, or other health programmes will become many times more effective. Since an estimated 80 percent of the immune tissue resides in the intestines, cleansing the colon from immune suppressive toxic waste and removing gallstones from the liver can make all the difference in the treatment of cancer, heart disease, AIDS, or other serious illnesses.

14.Dissolving Kidney Stones

If gallstones in the liver or other causes have led to the development of sand or stones in the kidneys or bladder (see "Urinary Disorders," Chapter 2), the kidneys need to be cleansed as well before recovery can be complete. The following are several herbs which, when taken daily over a period of about 20-30 days can help dissolve and eliminate all types of kidney stones, including uric acid stones, oxalic acid stones, phosphate stones, and amino acid stones. If you have a history of kidney stones, you may need to repeat this cleanse a few times at intervals of six weeks before the kidneys are completely clean.

Marjoran
Cat's Claw
Fennel Seed
Chicory Herb
Lemon Seed (if available)
Dried Uva Ursi
Hydrangea Root
Gravel root
Marshmallow root
Golden Rod Herb
Comfrey Root

Take equal amounts (2-3 ounces) of each of these roots and herbs and thoroughly mix them together. Keep in airtight container. Before bedtime, soak 3-4 heaped tablespoons (1/4 cup) of the mixture in two cups of water and leave covered overnight. The next morning bring it to boil, then let it simmer to 10-15 minutes and strin. Drink a few sips at a time in 6-8 portions throughout the day. It doesn't have to be taken warm or hot, but do not refrigerate. Don't add sugar or sweeteners. Leave at least one hour after eating before taking your next sips.

Repeat this procedure for 20-30 days. Make sure to drink at least 8 glasses of filtered water during the day. If you experience disconfort or stiffness in the lower back area it is because of salt crystals from kidnet stones passing through the ureter ducts of the unrinary system. Any strong smell of darkening of the urine at the beginning of the cleanse indicates a major release of toxins from the kidneys. Support the kidneys by drinking extra amounts of water, at least 6-8 glasses. During the cleanse, avoid consuming animalproducts, dairly foods, tea, coffee, alcohol, carbonatedbeverages, chocolate, and ant other foods or drink that contain preservatives, artifical sweeteners and coloring agents, etc. Each day chew 30-40 times on a small piece of rind from an organic lemon on the left side of your mouth and a small piece of carrot on the right side of your mouth. Make certain that there is at least half an hour in between.

15. Taking Liver Herbs

There are a number of herbs that can further improve liver performance and keep it nourished and vital. They can be made into a concoction and are best taken as a tea for ten days during each seasonal change or at times of acute illness. Although there are many herbs that help liver function and maintain clean blood, these are the most prominent ones.

Dandelion root
Comfrey root
Licorice root
Agrimony
Wild yam root
Barberry bark
Bearsfoot
Tanners oak bark
Milk thistle herb

For maximum effectiveness it is best to use all these herbs, if possible. Mix them together (in equal parts). Add ¼ cup of this mixture to one litre of water. Bring to a boil and cover with a lid. Let sit for six hours or overnight, then strain. Drink 2 cups a day on an empty stomach.

Taken on its own, tea made from the bark of the *red lapacho tree* which is also known as *Pau d'Arco, Ipe Roxa and Taheebo*, has *powerful* effects on the liver and immune system. The American Indian herb *Chaparral*, although tasting very bitter, is also an excellent liver and blood purifier.

16. Terminating Allergies

Although the liver cleanse helps remove the main causes of allergies in the body, it may take time before the cells of the immune system stop producing antibodies against antigens contained in certain foods, medicines, insect bites, mites of pillow feathers, air, or the environment. Antigens are foreign proteins, which stimulate a hypersensitive immune system to produce antibodies in order to deal with these, normally harmless, invaders. Non-microbial antigens may cause inflammation of nasal mucosa, nasal congestion, redness and itchiness of eyes, watery nose, and excessive secretion of tears. Subsequent contact with the same antigens leads to widening of capillary walls, hypersecretion of glands, and swelling of tissues.

Allergic reactions may also occur in the internal organs of the body, but because they are less obvious there, they are rarely associated with allergies. Allergic reactions which may have had their root cause in a congested liver and impaired digestive system, may thus be responsible for causing gallstones and even be the trigger for new illnesses, including arthritis, heart disease or cancer. One of the most effective methods to stop the body overreacting to such normally harmless antigens as found in dust, pollen, duck feathers, cats hair, or foods such as milk, wheat, mint, oranges, tomatoes, as well as to microbes that are amply present in our environment, is *Bio-resonance Therapy* – a method of "Vibrational Medicine."

It is known that every person suffering an illness or long-term complaint has one or several major allergies. An allergy results when repeated exposure of the body to a normally harmless substance or antigen stimulates the immune system to produce antibodies. In whichever part of the body the most antibodies are formed by local immune cells that is where the symptoms of disruption will occur more than in other parts. If it is in the nose, sinus cavities, or chest area, mucous congestion may arise. A similar response in an ovary or the prostate may lead to cysts or enlargement. In some instances, the reaction may cause anaphylactic shock, nausea, skin rashes, breathing difficulties, fainting, diarrhoea, and death.

There are four main allergies (which cover all other possible allergies). They involve the body's reactions to *duck feathers, milk, wheat, and mint*. If you happen to be allergic to duck feathers you may also be allergic to numerous allergens belonging to the same category as duck feathers, including, for example, certain dust particles, foods, metals, pollutants, etc. There may, in fact, be dozens of such substances. By annulling your body's allergic response to duck feathers through *Bio-resonance Therapy*, all these allergies will disappear as well. Similarly, when a wheat allergy is removed, the body's immune system will stop reacting to the antigens that fall into the wheat category. The same principle applies to the milk and mint allergy groups.

Most people with health problems have at least one of the four major allergies, which may, for example, be to wheat and its subordinates. Almost everyone who has teeth fillings with mercury-containing amalgam is allergic to milk, as well as to its products and its subordinates. Most cancer patients have allergies to three of the four main allergy groups. Independent research has shown that AIDS patients who have been tested for all the four allergy categories, are allergic to each of them which also means to numerous other substances. There may, indeed, hardly be a food, a chemical, a microbe (bacteria or virus) or a particle in the environment, which the body of an AIDS patient can still tolerate. Most other substances produce constant allergic reactions until the immune system is utterly exhausted and the patient dies from one or several opportunistic infections (AIDS diseases).

Bio-resonance therapists who test all major parts of the body the body for existing allergies and also each energy centre (chakra), seem to have very encouraging results. Subsequent tests after therapy show no further allergies to anything. The results are perpetuated when the liver, colon and kidneys are kept clean and a balanced diet and lifestyle is an integral part of daily life.

Recent research conducted in Germany on the value of *Bio-resonance Therapy* in the treatment of the severest forms of allergy showed that of 200 tested patients 83% were completely cured of all allergies and 11% had improved significantly. Although *Bio-resonance therapy* is effective even without a liver cleanse, the benefits are many times more pronounced if it is done after cleansing the liver. Each person will be able to prove for himself that his allergies have ceased when coming into contact with former antigens such as orange juice, milk, pollen, goose feathers or gluten as contained in wheat products, etc., without having an adverse reaction.

17. Replace all Metal Tooth Fillings

Metal dental ware is a constant source of poisoning and allergic reaction in the body. All metal corrodes in time, especially in the mouth where there is a high concentration of air and moisture. Mercury amalgam fillings release their extremely toxic compounds and vapour into the body, a reason why German dentists are prohibited by law to give them to pregnant women.

If mercury is considered dangerous for mother and baby, it must be considered dangerous for everyone. Particularly the liver and kidneys, which have to deal with noxious substances such as those released by metal filings, become gradually poisoned, impairing their functions. Cadmium, for example, which is used to make the pink colour in dentures, is five times as toxic as lead. It does not take much of it to raise the blood pressure to abnormal levels. Thallium, which is also found in mercury amalgam fillings, causes leg pain and paraplegia. It affects the nervous system, skin and cardiovascular system. All wheelchair patients who have been tested for metal poisoning tested positive for thallium. Many people who were in a wheelchair several years after they received metal fillings completely recovered after removing all metal from the mouth. Thallium is lethal at a dose of 0.5-1,0 gram.

Other metals contained in metal fillings are known for their cancer-producing (carcinogenic) effects. They include nickel, which is used in gold crowns, braces and children's crowns. Chromium is also extremely carcinogenic. All metals corrode, (including gold, silver or platinum) and the body absorbs it. Women with breast cancer have often accumulated large amounts of dissolved metals in their breasts. When the mouth is cleared of all metals, they will also leave the breasts and the cysts will shrink and disappear by themselves.

The body's immune system naturally responds to the presence of toxic metals in the body and eventually develops allergic reactions, which may show up as a sinus condition, tinnitus, enlarged neck and glands, bloating, enlarged spleen, arthritic conditions, headaches and migraine, eye diseases and more serious complications such as paralysis or heart attacks. An obvious way to improve these conditions is to replace all metal fillings with *plastic fillings* that contain *no* metals, cleanup the liver and kidneys and stop all allergic reactions through the *Bio-resonance Therapy* as described above.

18. The Use of Ener-Chi Art

Ener-Chi Art is a unique method of rejuvenation that helps to restore a balanced flow of Chi (vital energy) through the organs and systems in the body. When seen in the context of the liver cleanse, I consider this healing approach to be a very basic and useful tool in facilitating a successful outcome of other natural healing methods. When Chi flows again through the cells of the body, they can remove toxic wastes better, absorb all the oxygen, water, and nutrients they need, do the necessary repair work and increase their health and vitality. Although I consider the liver cleanse to be one of the most effective tools to help the body return to balanced functioning, by itself it may not be able to restore its overall vital energy due to many years of congestion and deterioration. Test results have shown that Ener-Chi Art may very well fill this gap. Its rate of effectiveness so far has been 100% for every person who has been exposed to it. (For more information on *Ener-Chi Art* see "Other Books and Products by the Author" at the end of this book.)

Chapter 7

Questions and Answers

The following are the most frequently asked questions and their answers with regard to gallstones and the liver cleanse.

Q. Isn't it natural or even advantageous to have a certain amount of gallstones in the liver?

A. Certainly not. Bile ducts are there to transport bile from the liver towards the intestinal tract similar to water pipes delivering water to a home. There is no advantage from having them blocked up. Since bile also carries toxins out of the liver, congested bile ducts obstruct this vital function, damaging the liver and leading to overall toxicity in the body.

Q. I am pregnant, is it OK for me to do the liver cleanse?

A. Although the liver has no known side effects on mother and baby, to be on the safe side, it is better to postpone the liver cleanse until 6 weeks after delivery. For future pregnancies, however, it is recommended to be gallstone-free before conception. This will ensure optimum health for both mother and baby during and after pregnancy.

Q. I cannot tolerate apple juice. Is there an alternative?

A. Apple juice seems to have the best properties to prepare the liver and gall bladder to expel gallstones easily and effectively. Try to drink it very slowly and/or water it down. If you cannot tolerate apple juice you can substitute with 200 ml of freshly squeezed lemon juice mixed with 800 ml of pure fresh water. Add 1 cm (½ inch) of grated ginger or ½ tsp. of ground ginger. Follow the same directions as given for drinking the apple juice.

Q. Would it be better to do the liver cleanses in intervals of two weeks or spread them over a longer period of time, say one every 2-3 months?

A. It's up to you to decide. After a liver cleanse, it takes from a few days up to two weeks before enough gallstones have moved from the rear of the liver towards the two hepatic ducts (exiting the liver) to make another purge worthwhile. You may want to do the cleanse every two weeks until no more stones come out or else take more time between each cleanse. If you do it every two weeks, start drinking the apple juice two weeks after the main purge. In any case, it is important that you get rid of *all* the stones, big and small. Just a few small ones clustered together at one of the larger bile ducts can produce major symptoms of discomfort in the body, such as indigestion, bloating, headache, backache, etc.

Q. Shall I avoid doing a liver cleanse while I am menstruating?

A. Although the liver cleanse is also effective when done during the menstrual period it is more convenient for women to cleanse their liver before or after the period. Besides, menstrual bleeding is a form of cleansing and it is best for the body not to cleanse at two ends at the same time.

Q. Is it really necessary to have a colonic irrigation before and after each liver cleanse?

A. For optimum results, the liver cleanse should always be preceded and followed by some form of colonic cleansing. The quickest and most reliable method of freeing the colon of spastic or obstructed areas is colonic irrigation. Once the colonic therapist tells you that your colon is clean, you can skip the colonics before the liver cleanses but continue having them after the liver cleanses, ideally within three days. The colonic eliminates any gallstones that may have been trapped in the colon [the experience tells that there are always some stones left behind, which could become a source of irritation or inflammation]. If you don't have the opportunity for a colonic irrigation, apply any other method of colon cleansing, such as herbal cleansers, oxygen treatments, or enemas (although they tend to cleanse only the lower part of the colon). Still, I don't recommend you to use the liver cleanse without having a colonic afterwards.

Q. I have had three liver cleanses so far and eliminated a total of about 900-1000 stones of all sizes and colours. Most stones came out during the second and third cleanses. When is my liver going to improve?

A. Your liver functions started improving the moment the first stones were expelled. Gallstones congesting the liver bile ducts have a suffocating effect on surrounding liver cells. Releasing the stones through the liver cleanse helps them "breathe" again, produce more bile and detoxify the blood more efficiently. Although the larger bile ducts keep blocking up again as the smaller bile ducts pass their stones into them, eventually they are also cleared (through repeated cleansing). Once all stones have been removed the liver as whole can repair itself and restore normal functions.

Q. How long does it take to receive the full benefits from completing a series of lets say six liver cleanses?

A. Once your liver has released the last gallstones, the digestive functions will improve significantly, which will benefit every part of the body. This also gives the rest of the body the opportunity to cleanse itself and repair the damage that has occurred due to the accumulation of gallstones in the liver and gall bladder. Any cleansing reactions that may result from the removal of the stones are to be viewed as positive side effects. If other causes of ill health have been eliminated as well (as explained in chapter 6), this phase will be short-lived and be replaced by a new sense of well being and vitality. Normally, it may take up to six month before all liver functions have returned to normal. Having a clean liver is one of the best guarantees for a disease-free life.

Q. I am 76 years old and suffer from osteoporosis, digestive trouble and several other ailments. Can anyone at my age still benefit from the liver cleanse?

A. Age is no impediment for the body to be healthy. As long as your liver is alive, so long can a liver cleanse help you improve its functions and through that, increase the nutrient and energy supply to the cells of the body. The negative aspect of ageing is just a progressive state of malnutrition and toxicity, both of which can be helped with a series of liver cleanses. The elderly respond very well to the liver cleanse and show increased signs of energy, physical mobility, clarity of mind, appetite, sensory enjoyment, and a better sense of self. Apart from improving their physical and mental condition, they often report of *"coming to life again."* No elderly person should to die from a debilitating disease. If the liver cleanse could be introduced into old age homes it could help restore the people's health, dignity and self-sufficiency and perhaps even start off a new phase of life for them.

Q. Ultrasound scans have shown that I have a fatty liver. My whole body is swollen and I have several lumps in my breasts and my thyroid. My blood cholesterol is very high and I frequently throw up. Could the liver cleanse help?

A. There is no medical therapy to date that can remove fat deposits from the liver. But you can prove to yourself and to your doctor that you can reduce and even eliminate all fatty deposits in the liver by clearing the liver's bile ducts of all gallstones. The liver may have accumulated these deposits because of many reasons, such as high protein, sugar, and alcohol consumption, or stress. Whatever the reason or reasons may have been to contribute towards developing a congested liver, by cleansing your liver repeatedly it will gradually improve and repair itself to whatever extent possible. Take another scan after your sixth liver cleanse and let your doctor compare it with the previous one. The difference will be black against white. Once your liver is cleared of fatty deposits, they will also disappear from other parts of the body, i.e. breasts, thyroid, arteries, etc. This is, provided you maintain a balanced, low protein, preferably vegetarian diet and moderate lifestyle.

Q. Can taking Epsom salts have any side effects?

A. So long as the liver is congested, Epsom salts – in combination with olive oil and grapefruit juice -- have no harmful effects. After the liver has been cleared of all stones, in order to avoid possible irritation, it is not necessary to cleanse more often than twice a year. For a similar reason, once your colon is completely clean, which may be the case after a series of colonic irritations, you may reduce the dose of the last two helpings of Epsom salts to half. This also applies when during your previous liver cleanse the last 5-6 bowel movements in the morning or afternoon consisted merely of water without any stones or white cholesterol segments. If you are totally intolerant to Epsom salts, try other natural colonic cleansers that work fast, like the American product *Colosan*, which consists of a blend of various magnesium oxides. *Colosan* can be purchased from American company *The Family Health News*, Florida, 9845 N.E 2nd Avenue, Miami Shores, Fl 33138; Tel. 1-800-284-6263 or 305-759-9500. The disadvantage with most other colon cleansers is that, unlike Epsom salts, they don't open the bile ducts to release the gallstones into the intestinal tract – an essential part of the cleanse.

Q. Is any type of olive oil suitable for the liver cleanse?

A. The olive oil should be cold pressed and 100% pure. Usually olive oil that bears the label "Extra Virgin Olive Oil" is the best but nevertheless read the small text. It should state that this oil has not been mixed with other oils. Unfortunately, in some countries, olive oil is sold as extra virgin but contains 80% Soya oil. If you are not sure about its authenticity, test it out with the *Kinesiology* muscle test. There are many books or videotapes available that can help you apply this simple method of testing; it tells you immediately whether a product is suitable for you or not. There is also an exact description of the testing procedure in the book "The Perfect Health Guide."

Q. I am taking food supplements. Should I continue taking them while doing the liver cleanse?

A. It is best to avoid any supplements or medicines during the cleanse, unless they are absolutely essential. Besides, they are wasted as they are flushed out with the Epsom salts. Besides, medicinal drugs and substances like sleeping pills have a suppressive effect which can render the cleanse ineffective.

Q. I have done eight liver cleanses so far and I feel great. Almost all of my symptoms including stomach ulcers, sinusitis, and headaches are gone without a trace. In total I must have released about 2,500 stones. What I don't understand is why my first liver cleanse produced no stones whatsoever and the second one only 6-7 small ones. During the following cleanse I passed about a thousand, much to my amazement. Can you explain why I wasn't successful with the firsts two cleanses?

A. You are one of the rare people whose major liver bile in the liver must have been solidly congested with gallstones and it took three cleanses to soften the hardened structures and break them down. It is not true that the first two cleanses weren't successful, they were. They did the groundwork or digging and the following cleanses just removed what was dug up. Thanks to your persistence!

Concluding Remarks

Cleansing the liver is not something that has been invented recently. The ancient cultures knew of the necessity to keep the liver clean. There are plenty of useful cleansing formulas around that were handed down through the generations either by ancestral education or traditional healers. Although the exact mechanisms of these cleansing procedures were not known then as they are today (through the methods of scientific understanding and investigation), they are still valid, scientific and effective. Medical science still has to come to terms with the fact that there are numerous useful methods of healing that have worked for millions of people throughout the ages and that can make all the difference in the treatment of the most threatening diseases that plague our modern societies.

Every house or appliance requires some form of maintenance or repair work from time to time, otherwise it will lose the purpose it was designed for. This also applies to the liver, since there is no other organ in the body besides the brain that is so complex and has so many vital functions. We clean our teeth and wash our skin because we know that exposure to food, air, chemicals etc., tends to leave residues that can make us feel unclean and uncomfortable. Not many people, however, think that the same principle of cleaning applies to the inside of the body as well. The lungs, skin intestines, kidneys, and the liver deal with a tremendous amount of internally produced waste, which is a necessary by-product of breathing, digestion and metabolism in the body.

Under normal circumstances, i.e., when eating nutritious and organic foods, living in a pollution free environment, having plenty of physical movement and exercise, living a balanced lifestyle, etc., the body can properly take care of the daily arising metabolic waste products and eliminate them safely from the system. This situation changes, however, when our diet, lifestyle, and environment are no longer balanced enough to suit the body's requirements for energy, nourishment and flawless circulation. One of the organs that suffer the most from an overload of toxic chemicals, poor quality of food, lack of exercise, etc. is the liver. Hence it is of utter importance for every person who is concerned about his health to ensure that his liver is cleared of any obstructions and weaknesses.

Cleansing the liver is not something someone can do for you. It is rather a self-help-method that requires a profound sense of self-responsibility and trust in the wisdom of the body. You will only feel drawn towards cleansing your liver when you know deep within yourself that this is something you absolutely have to do. If you don't feel this way put this book aside and wait. When the time is right, you will feel the definite impulse or desire to improve your liver's functions.

Although the liver cleanse is not a cure for diseases, it sets the precondition for the body to heal itself. In fact, there rarely is a disease that cannot be significantly helped by improving liver performance. To understand the great significance of the liver cleanse one needs to experience for oneself how it feels to have a liver that has been relieved of two hands full of gallstones. For many people, the liver cleanse has been an "amazing" experience, reason enough to share it with those willing to help themselves.

Other Books and Products
by the Author

"The Key to Health and Rejuvenation"
(*see note below)

This book meets the increasing demand for a clear and comprehensive guide that can make a person self-sufficient regarding his health and well being. The presentation answers some of the most pressing questions of our time: How does illness arise? Who heals, who doesn't? Are we destined to be sick? What causes ageing, is it reversible? What are the major causes of disease and how can we eliminate them?

Topics included are: The placebo and the mind/body mystery; The laws of illness and health; The four most common risk factors of disease; Digestive disorders and their effects on the rest of the body; Wonders of our biological rhythms and how to restore them if disrupted; How to create a life of balance; Why choose a vegetarian diet; Cleansing the liver, gall bladder, kidneys and colon; Removing allergies; Giving up smoking naturally; Using sunlight as medicine; The "new" causes of heart disease, cancer, and AIDS; Antibiotics, blood transfusions, ultrasounds scans, immunisation programmes under scrutiny;

"The Key to Health and Rejuvenation" sheds light on all the major issues of health care and reveals that most medical treatments, including surgery, blood transfusions, drugs, etc., are avoidable when certain key functions in the body are restored through the natural methods described in the book. The reader also learns about the potential dangers of medical diagnosis and treatment and the reasons vitamin supplements, 'health' foods, light products, "wholesome" breakfast cereals, diet foods and diet programmes may have contributed to the current health crisis rather than helped resolve it. The book includes a complete

programme of health care, which is primarily based on the ancient medical system of Ayurveda.

*"It's Time to Wake Up" (*see note below)*

In this book the author brings to light man's deep inner need for spiritual wisdom in life and helps the reader develop a new sense of reality that is based on love, power and compassion. He describes in detail our relationship with the natural world and how we can harness its tremendous powers for our personal and mankind's benefit. "It's Time to Wake Up" challenges some of our most commonly held beliefs and offers a way out of the restrictions and limitations we have created in our lives.

Topics include: What shapes our Destiny; Using the power of intention; Secrets of defying the ageing process; Doubting -- the cause of failure; Opening the heart; Material wealth and spiritual wealth; Fatigue – the major cause of stress; Methods of emotional transformation; Techniques of primordial healing; How to increase health of the 5 senses; Developing spiritual wisdom; The major causes of today's earth changes; Entry into the new world; Twelve gateways to heaven on earth; and many more.

*Note: Both these books are available in printed and bound form and as electronic books on the Internet. They electronic versions may be downloaded into a computer from the publisher's website, **www1stbooks.com** .

The book "The Key to Health and Rejuvenation" used to run under the title "The Key to Perfect Health."

Ener-Chi Art

In collaboration with Dr. Lillian Maresch, Andreas Moritz has developed a new system of healing and rejuvenation that is designed to restore the basic life energy (Chi) of an organ or a system in the body, within a matter of minutes. Simultaneously, it also helps balance the emotional causes of illness.

Eastern approaches to healing, such as Acupuncture and Shiatsu, are intended to enhance well-being by stimulating and balancing the flow of Chi to the various organs and systems of the body. In a similar manner, the energetics of Ener-Chi Art are designed to restore a balanced flow of Chi throughout the body.

According to most ancient systems of health and healing, the balanced flow of Chi is the key determinant for a healthy body and mind. When Chi flows through the body unhindered, health and vitality are maintained. By contrast, if the flow of Chi is disrupted or reduced, health and vitality tend to decline.

A person can determine the degree to which the flow of Chi is balanced in the body's organs and systems by using a simple muscle testing procedure. To reveal the effectiveness of Ener-Chi Art, it is important to apply this test both before and after viewing each Ener-Chi Art picture.

To allow for easy application of this system, Andreas has created a number of healing paintings that have been "activated" through a unique procedure that imbues each work of art with specific colour rays. To receive the full benefit of an Ener-Chi Art picture all that is necessary is to look at it for about two minutes. During this time, the flow of Chi within the organ or system becomes fully restored. When applied to all the organs and systems of the body, Ener-Chi Art sets the precondition for the whole body to self-heal and rejuvenate in their its own time.

To order individual prints or complete sets of these pictures contact the address below.

For further information contact:

Ener-Chi Unlimited
P.O. Box 52
Excelsior, Minnesota 55331
USA

Fax: +1-612-470- 9889
E-mail: EnerChiArt@aol.com

ABOUT THE AUTHOR

Andreas Moritz is a health consultant and practitioner of Ayurvedic Medicine. Born in Southwest Germany in 1954, Andreas had to deal with several severe illnesses from an early age, which compelled him to study diet, nutrition, and various methods of natural healing while still a child.

By the age of 20 he had completed his training in iridology - the diagnostic science of eye interpretation - and dietetics. A year later he qualified as a teacher of meditation. In 1981 he began studying Ayurvedic Medicine in India and completed his training as a qualified practitioner of Ayurveda in New Zealand in 1991. Andreas has had particular success with cases of terminal disease where conventional methods of healing were futile. Since 1988, he has been practising the Japanese healing art of Shiatsu, which has given him profound insights into the energy system of the body. In addition, he devoted eight years of active research into consciousness and its important role in the field of mind/body medicine.

Andreas Moritz is also the author of "The Amazing Liver Cleanse" and "It's Time to Wake Up." During his extensive travels throughout the world he has consulted heads of state and members of governments in Europe, Asia, and Africa, and has lectured widely on the subject of health and mind/body medicine. He is currently involved in developing a new system of healing and rejuvenation - *Ener-Chi Art* - that can help restore the vital energy flow of organs and systems in the body.

Printed in the United States
1627